My Grandmother's Faith

The Outcome of Unconditional Love

by Rodney Dean Boyden

Illustrated by Rodney Dean Boyden

ARC Communications, LLC Editorial Coordinator:
Richard W. Griffin, Ph.D., (Texas A&M University, 1991)

Copyright © 2016 Rodney Dean Boyden

All rights reserved. No part of this publication may be reproduced, stored in a retrieval system, or transmitted in any form or by any means without the written permission of the publisher.

Published by ARC Communications, LLC
P. O. Box O
College Station, Texas 77841
Email: arccommunications@arc-culturalart.com

Cover by MT GRAPHIX

ISBN-13: 978-0-9909046-8-7
ISBN-10: 0-9909046-8-7

Printed in the USA

Table of Contents

Acknowledgments v
The Editor's Note ix
Prologue xiii
Chapter One: Happiness is Tea
    and Chicken Wings 17
Chapter Two: The Handshake 33
Chapter Three: Location of Validation 43
Chapter Four: My Safety Net 53
Chapter Five: The Day I Walked Away 65
Chapter Six: Mind Regulator 83
Chapter Seven: The Great Debate 97
Chapter Eight: Thriving Behind the Scenes 123
Chapter Nine: Attitude Under Pressure 143
Chapter Ten: Mind, Material and Machine 165
Chapter Eleven: "Why Me? Why Music?" 177
Chapter Twelve: Mamma's Legacy 193
Epilogue: Finding Normal 203
Dear Mamma 214
Had I Not Been 220
Biography 223

List of Hymns

Give Me A Clean Heart 31
If I Can Help Somebody 42
Higher Ground 52
My Hope is Built on Nothing Less 63
"Without God, I Could Do Nothing" 82
Farther Along 96
Lead Me, Guide Me 109
This Little Light of Mine 142
Glory, Glory 163
How Great Thou Art 176
Jesus is All the World to Me 191
I Surrender All 212
You Who Brought Me Love 218

My Grandmother's Faith

Acknowledgments

Writing this book has been an experience unlike any other. It has caused me to reach back and think of all who were instrumental in the development of who I am today.

I extend special thanks to all of you who shared and undergirded the love that my grandmother gave me through your many acts of kindness throughout the years.

Mr. Lawrence W. Boyden (deceased)
Mrs. Doris J. McCormick and Family
Mr. Dennis L. Boyden and Family
Dr. Cassandra M. Kirkpatrick
Mr. & Mrs. Christopher and Lisa Kirkpatrick & Family
Mr. & Mrs. James and Betty Spencer & Family
Bishop T.D. Jakes and First Lady Serita Jakes & Family
Mr. Tyler Perry

~~~

Ms. Wanda Albritton & Family
Mrs. Ethel Caffie Austin
Mrs. Angela Sanders Bentley & Family
Ms. Terri Berkley
Ms. Judy Slade Bolin
The Boyden Family
Rev. & Mrs. Robert I. (deceased) and Sheila Brown & Family
Ms. Arlene Burke & Family
Mr. Sherman (deceased) and Betty Charlton & Family
Mrs. Ida Mae Crawford & Family
Mr. Rodney Cross
Ms. Akema Johnson Day & Family
Mr. & Mrs. Robert Dobson & Family
The Dooley Family

Rodney Dean Boyden

The Families and Friends of Dunbar-Institute, WV
Mr. Eric Foxx
Mr. & Mrs. Kirk and Tammy Franklin
Bishop & Mrs. Clifford and Pamela Frazier & Family
Mr. & Mrs. Jesse and Regina Gibbs & Family
Mr. & Mrs. Dale and Vernette Gilbreath & Family
Mr. & Mrs. Jack and Sarah Griffith
Mr. & Mrs. Winfred and Mary Harris & Family
Mr. & Mrs. George and Debbie Hart
Mrs. Sandre Henderson & Family
Rev. & Mrs. E. Alphonso Heyliger & Family
Mr. & Mrs. Dale and Genoa Jackson & Family
Ms. Robin Jenkins & Family
Mr. & Mrs. Floyd and Charlotte Jones & Family
Ms. Jacquetta Johnson & Family
Mrs. Lauretha Kellum
Mr. Quincy Madison
Mr. Jeff Massie (deceased) & Family
LTC Robert H. (deceased) and Mrs. Stella Meggison & Family
Mr. & Mrs. Clabon (deceased) and Shirley Pleasant & Family
Mr. & Mrs. Willie (deceased) and Dorothy Peoples & Family
Ms. Judy Peterson
Rev. & Mrs. C. J. R. and Esther Phillips & Family
Mr. & Mrs. Joseph and Stephanie Phillips & Family
Ms. Angie Richardson & Family
Ms. Daryl Richardson & Family
Mrs. Bessie Smoot (deceased)
Ms. Pam M. Smith (and Zoee)
Ms. Shawnte Spencer and Jayla Johnson
The Peaks & Staunton Family
Mr. Jay Tillman & Family
Mr. Daryl Waldrop

My Grandmother's Faith

Ms. Andrea Wallace and Son Preston Wallace & Family
West Virginia State University

Cascade United Methodist Church
Central Baptist Church
Ferguson Memorial Baptist Church
First Baptist Church Huntington
Hamilton Park United Methodist Church
Heartline Ministries
Morning Star Baptist Church
Shorter African Methodist Episcopal Church
Simpson United Methodist Church
St. Paul African Methodist Episcopal Church
St. Paul Baptist Church
The Potter's House Church

I would like to thank Dr. Richard W. Griffin of ARC Communications, LLC for his amazing ability to reel in my thoughts and push me to the completion of this project. I wish him continued success as he shares his company's Little Flower Literacy Project www.littleflowerartist.com and www.littleflowerdolls.com with the world. Had it not been for him, this book would not be a reality.

Rodney Dean Boyden

My Grandmother's Faith

The Editor's Note

The truly dedicated teacher works to educate every student who is interested in learning the subject matter. Obviously the task proves to be much more difficult if the student is not willing to be engaged in this whole process. Each student brings a unique set of abilities and potentialities to the classroom. The teacher must quickly conduct an assessment and formulate a plan to reach that place in the student's mind where the light bulb will burn brightly at the onset of the "I got it" moment. I liken a book editor to a teacher in the sense that the editor wishes to step into the mind of the writer and quickly determine the thread of connected knowledge that the author is interested in relaying to the reader. The editor must figure out how to interact with the author on a myriad of levels as related to style, voice, message, tone, and energy. Ultimately, after countless reviews, drafts, and edits, the final edited manuscript is placed in the hands or computer files of the proud author. I have never had any biological children. Nevertheless, I am a proud godparent and "academic" parent to hundreds of wonderful students who have allowed me to share a portion of my knowledge with them as I have spent the last 25 years in the hallowed halls of academia.

Have you ever been in the presence of a genius-level mind? How did you feel about your own abilities when you realized that the individual that you were conversing with either physically, telephonically, or digitally by computer was obviously thinking on a much higher-ordered plane than yourself? Well, imagine my surprise when Rodney Dean Boyden effortlessly rattled off hours of stories about growing up with his grandmother. As an editor, it was my job to put forth my very best effort to begin and continue a structured dialogue, as part of the work effort, with this multi-talented anomalous human being. Although I have exchanged dialogue with many scholars during the course of my life and career, I have never encountered one who thinks so freely, without any limitations in either left- or right-brain mode. Yes, my editing game was instantly challenged, because Rodney was literally running in mental circles around my mind as I attempted to formulate a plan to structure the editorial process of this book from inception to completion. Still, I had no fear, as others had crossed this same bridge while guiding brilliant authors. I remembered even Einstein and others that exist in the constellation of geniuses (bright minds) had once been guided from concept to finished document. I am very glad that I forged ahead with the *My Grandmother's Faith* plan of action.

Rodney embodies the ideals of the Renaissance man and he freely converses across a wide range of topics. All I had to do was ask a question, which sparked a conversation that meandered for hundreds of hours. In the end, his point was made and I was left wiser and smarter for taking a few months of my time to walk down that path with an endowed thinker who tested me at every turn, determined to get me to see his point of view.

I am blessed to have been afforded an opportunity to work with this exciting author who wishes to enlighten the global society with his brilliant stories and insights. Rodney's first book, *My Grandmother's Faith*, offers a new testimonial of God's Faithfulness. It is my prayer that it will be a blessing to readers in all walks of life. I thank you, Mamma Boyden, for a life well lived. Your faith has encouraged us all.

ARC Communications, LLC Editorial Coordinator:
Richard W. Griffin, Ph.D., (Texas A&M University, 1991)

Prologue

Long ago, I reached the conclusion that my true self is "Creative," which alone explains who I am and why I am uniquely me. I surmised that at some point, God decided to make creative people to enable the world to do, have, and experience, new things. Coming into this realization relieved some of the pressure off of me just being free to be me, and gave me a bit of solace in knowing that I am not crazy after all. Like many creative people all over the world, I live in a space that most people just can't understand, because it goes against the grain of normalcy. This way of life causes me to just act strange and to do strange things, while on the path to wherever my creativity takes me.

In March of 2014, the Huffington Post ran an article titled "18 Things Highly Creative People Do Differently" and, while closely studying each of the article's 18 points, I saw myself. At that moment, I realized that the habits I had long thought of as flaws are closely associated with creative thinking and these same habits are actually stable, defining characteristics in some personalities similar to my own. Like other creative types, I daydream, I observe everything, I work the hours that work for me, I take time for solitude, I turn around life's obstacles, I seek out new experiences, I "Fail" up, I ask the BIG questions, I people watch, I take risks, I view all life as an opportunity for self expression, I follow my passion, I get out of my own head, I lose track of time, I surround myself with beauty, I connect the dots that nobody else connects, I constantly shake up things, and I make time for mindfulness.

Yes, that is definitely me. The creative guy known as Rodney Dean Boyden and, at the time of this writing, I am in my 50th year of this gift we call life. While I imagine that turning 50 years old affects everyone differently, this half-century milestone was a highly anticipated birthday for me that commenced with a wonderful black-tie party event, attended by many of my closest family members and friends. The party was grand!

A couple of months following the party, I had a life changing epiphany that caused me to think about my life as a whole. Through this stroll down memory lane, I realized that my grandmother set all of my life's positive events in motion. This new revelation inspired me to dissect who I am as an individual and to closely

My Grandmother's Faith

analyze why I do what I do. This process has also challenged me to critically examine the ups and downs and positives and negatives of all of the talents and skills that I possess. The outcome of this soul-searching journey is reflected through the short stories that are shared in this book. I am grateful to God for the gift of my deceased grandmother, Mrs. Pauline C. Boyden; for the gift of my grandmother's faith; for the gift of my own faith; and for the gift of my God-given talents.

Several of the book's chapters were written in a cemetery. I don't mean to sound morbid, but one of the most beautiful military cemeteries in the world is located in my home state of West Virginia. The cemetery is maintained and kept in pristine condition and each of my many visits there lifted my spirits and helped me to reflect on my past, while illuminating a bright future filled with endless possibilities. I chose this place, because it was one of the few places that gave me the silence and uninterrupted solitude that I needed to think through it all. On occasion, when I was the cemetery's only visitor, I mused that I was the only one there who had a chance to change existing circumstances. It seemed as if the souls, whose names were represented on the marble tombstones, understood and supported the real-time reality that their time had passed, but I still had time, as the poet William Wordsworth said, "to learn from the past, profit from the present, and to live better in the future." The tranquility of this uniquely chosen environment inspired me to share my truth in a manner that I trust will encourage others to seek a deeper understanding of themselves and the work that they were born into this lifetime to complete.

    The stories in this book are based on my life's experiences and are told from my perspective. Like an erupting volcano, they came forth, uninhibited, from the deepest trenches of my heart and soul. They represent the good and the bad of what makes **<u>me</u>** the person that I am. The stories unearthed recollections of soul-stirring events in my life and awakened emotions of deep laughter, poignant regret, burning tears, powerful dreams, critical introspection, and an overflowing of gratitude that surpassed anything that I had ever experienced in life. All said, I am thankful for this opportunity to share a few glimpses into the bond between my grandmother and myself, as well as, the power and legacy of her faith in God and in me.

Chapter One: Happiness is Tea and Chicken Wings

My bond with my grandmother began at birth. My grandparents, Lawrence and Pauline C. Boyden, whom I refer to as Mamma and Daddy, adopted me immediately after I was born and provided me with a secure, memorable, dreamlike, childhood. My birth mother, who is my Grandmother's only daughter, was a college student when I was born. She was never far away and always a part of my life.

From my earliest recollections, Daddy worked in New York and, while he took care of my Mamma and me financially, he was not physically present with us most of the time, so Mamma was my primary caregiver.

First and foremost, in my mind and in my heart, Mamma was a lady. Also, she was the love of my life and a woman of great faith in God and in me. My grandmother's faith was unquestionably tied to the beautiful, long-suffering, loving, caring, and giving heart that she possessed inside of her sturdy frame. She loved from a "heart" place that corralled a range of feelings and emotions that enabled her to be wide and vast in her thought processes and actions. Mamma knew a lot and gave a lot, even when it did not benefit her directly.

When I tell my friends that I am looking for a lady to be my wife, and I give them my definition of a lady, they say that I am superficial. I do not consider my dream lady's qualities to be superficial, but I am aware of what a lady is, because I saw and loved one every day for nearly three decades. I believe that a lady is the epitome of the female situation, because she knows how to be everything. As they used to say, "she can bring home the bacon and fry it up in a pan." Mamma was one of those types and I watched her closely.

As we both readied ourselves for church, I noticed how she paid particular attention to her hair, and clothing, including suits and coordinated accessories of shoes, purses, gloves, and, we surely can't leave out, the hat. Also, I watched as she applied just a little powder to her face to smooth it out just a little bit. Then, she put that red stuff on her cheeks to make them a little rosy, but did not put on lip liner, eye shadow, and all that stuff. She was a lady and she was pretty enough that she did not need all of that, because "pretty is as pretty does."

Mamma had steel gray eyes and pretty hands that she protected with gloves while she cleaned or worked in her garden. She was a strong woman, not a pansy. She worked, walked, and knew how to take care of her obligations.

Mamma's faith was a faith on the move and faith in action! Born in 1913 in Philadelphia, PA, she was the youngest of four children, and graduated from Dubois High School in Mount Hope, WV. She was a faithful, tithing member, and choir member of the Central Baptist Church in Beckley, WV for over fifty years. She was a politically active community leader, who served as an active member of the Women's Improvement League and Modernistic Homemakers Club, as well as a local Committeewoman for the Republican Party. Mamma sang and played the piano, planted a garden every year, was an excellent cook, fried the best chicken, made the best fudge, fed the neighborhood all of the time, and could operate a coal furnace better than a man. Most importantly to me though, was, and is, the fact that MAMMA LOVED ME and understood the complexity of the diverse gifts that were bestowed upon me. She had the ability and patience to water my seeds of creativity, ingenuity, and innovation that would later blossom inside of me as I purposely moved along the Boulevard of Life. I was Mamma's and she was mine. She and I were inseparable. We were a pair. We were a team. I often say that Mamma never really taught me anything in particular, but she created an environment in which I could learn everything. And learn everything, I did.

Mamma was my archetype of Christ. The love, support and influence that she provided me, during my first twenty-seven years of life, inspired my unwavering faith in God and still guides me more than two decades after her physical departure from this earth. My grandmother died at the age of eighty, when I was twenty-seven years old. A huge part of me died with her.

For the last twenty-three years, the approach of Mother's Day has affected me in the same interesting way, because having loved and been loved by a sweet grandmother, who is no longer with me, is a very difficult thing. It seems as though my hearing goes silent, my vision goes dim, and the world becomes a place where I hear or see nothing on that day. I try my best to get through the day, get past it, and let it be something that is a faded memory, even though I know that the faded memory must be repeated annually.

Just as biblical stories tell about God and his acts in history for humanity's salvation, turning 50 years old caused me to examine the totality of my own humanity. In so doing, I gained a deeper appreciation for God's hand upon my life and His choice of Mamma as my life guide. The stories and analogies of the derivative fruit of my grandmother's faith have shaped my life as a multi-talented, creative, artist.

I am a musician, because, at an early age, Mamma asked me if I wanted to take piano lessons. When I responded yes, she hired a wonderful piano teacher to give me private lessons for many years, and she made sure that I practiced every night. On many evenings, when it was time for me to practice, Mamma would come to the door and holler in a high-pitched voice, RodNeeeeeeee!!! Upon hearing the familiar summons, my childhood playmates went home and I went inside to practice piano. Since Mamma was a pianist, she knew the importance of that skill and how mastering it would benefit me in the future. She accompanied me to nearly every lesson and she sat behind me reading her paper and books, just so that I could feel her presence in the room.

I am a tailor, because there was a sewing machine in the house. While Mamma never showed me anything about sewing, I learned to sew, because she allowed me the freedom to experiment and she appreciated the garments that resulted from my budding talent.

I am a singer, because Mamma always encouraged me to sing and provided me with the confidence needed to perform in front of large crowds of people. She taught me to stand erect, walk erect, sit erect, and to always dress immaculately for my performances.

I am a visual artist and a carpenter, because as a kid, I enjoyed creating things. Mamma always made sure that I had all of the supplies that I needed to complete my personal projects. These items included every color of construction paper, lots of tape, scissors, pencils, and markers. In addition to winning many drawing contests as a child, later in life, my career in construction also greatly benefited from techniques discovered during my childhood play, and rightfully so, since much of the construction trade is all about shapes. I can cut fabric and sew it together or cut wood and put it together. In my way of thinking, it's the exact same thing.

The multitude of varied skills that I learned by being around Mamma as a child and as a young adult allowed me to pursue career paths that have fulfilled my desire to be creative and connected to others for the sake of the artistic pursuit. I realize now that Mamma's love and guidance was an umbrella over my life and also served as a counterweight, which balanced my propensity towards mental overdrive. No matter what happened during the course of a day, when I drove up into Mamma's driveway, I knew that everything would be all right. Even as a man, I loved sitting beside Mamma and laying my head in her lap. I'll forever remember that when I laid my head in her lap and she ran her fingers through my hair, then all of the anxiety from that day's toils just floated away. I knew that, just for that one moment, I was back in the place where the touch of her hand, which was covered with a cloak of unconditional love, was wiping away the week's pain. Through this simple action, my pain was sifted through her soul and transferred back into me as undying love that would carry me, until I returned once again for a refill.

This kind of personal interaction with loved ones is very important, because out in the world, as we move throughout society, there are things that happen to us that are good and bad. We are just human beings fueled by various types of energy. Sometimes your energy level drains and even though you feel like you are doing well in life, you can still be worn out for a prolonged period of time. Then, sometimes in life, there are things that happen to you that just seem to pull on your ability to continue. It is not easy to have a lot of negative things happen in your life, because you have only a certain amount of energy that you get from just being alive. When bad things happen, in rapid fire succession, such as: you lose your job, the kids are going wild, your husband is going crazy, your wife is losing her mind, the church people are driving you nuts, your job is doing unnecessary stuff, and your friends are turning their backs on you, it pulls on your own ability to be sane. This will drag you down like nothing else that you've ever imagined.

Once again I was back in the place where love lived, love sat, and where this earthly love resides. It resided in a woman who had given her very life to me. Mamma's ever-steady presence meant more to me than I was able to fully understand at the time. Isn't it amazing what time and life can teach you about the infinite value of the simple truth of unconditional love?

Mamma passed away in 1993. It was on that day in that year that the governor in my brain disintegrated and my mental overdrive was no longer throttled. Now, twenty-three years later at fifty years old, I am still battling to calibrate the creative forces that drive me to pursue a menagerie of occupations in my creative space. "Are you happy?" was the question that someone recently asked me. " I am not happy," but "I am not unhappy either," was my response. An explanation for my answer comes with a unique set of twists and turns, with the true meaning suspended somewhere in between. Only one who comprehends the nature of a creative mind in mental overdrive can fully understand the meaning of this response.

Many people look at my appearance, listen to me sing and play the piano, appreciate my carpentry skills, view other short clips from my life, and surmise that my world is filled with wonderment, excitement, and all types of things that are great and good. They have no idea of what it is really like to live in this space, in this time, and in this mind. Oftentimes, it is a lonely and misunderstood existence. The mind of a creative person is always thinking, always creating, and always moving. During the day, my creative mind and my personal feelings and thoughts, all try to figure out which way I'm going to end up that day. What emotion(s) will I go to bed with that night? What emotion(s) will I fall asleep with? Additionally, many times when my body so desperately needs sleep, my mind will allow my eyes to close, but only for a moment. Just as my thoughts manage to slow down and I'm close to falling asleep, SIGNALS, like radio waves that have the longest wavelengths in the electromagnetic spectrum, awaken my mind again and thoughts race from subject to subject, until finally in the wee hours of the morning, I fall asleep.

I awaken each new day to find myself back on yet another track of wondering thoughts. What will the day bring? What surprise will present itself? What gift will I need to employ? What call will I receive? What question will I be asked? What opportunities will come my way out of the clear blue sky? One may think that this would be a fun and exciting existence, but actually it is complete and utter torment.

Happiness? Happiness! Happiness. The word happiness is defined differently depending upon the person defining it. However, two synonyms of the word that I aspire to reach are peace and contentment. This is my goal, because my happiness comes in spurts and it goes in spurts and it comes in spurts and it goes in spurts. Yes, I did repeat those words, because that's how it feels to be me, on any given day, and at any given time. When I allow myself to reflect on my life and some of the good thoughts come to mind, they are always perched on top of some of the less desirable thoughts. Each day as I walk, and talk, and work, and create, my mind dives into all of these emotions, which relentlessly pull me in many different directions.

It is the thought of happiness that eludes me. For it is my wish to one day be in one place, at one time, with one love, while enjoying all of my skills and talents at the same time. Anyone who befriends me for any amount of time will conclude that knowing me is to know my talents. That is where my happiness lies. My grandest wish has always been to obtain it. However, due to my creativity, opportunities just never stopped coming my way, and I never stopped searching for them.

A word to the wise, don't ever look at a person's appearance and overlook the inside of the person. For it is the inside that really matters. The inside of a person is the place where all of the work is done. The inside of a person is the place where all of the fights happen. The inside of a person is the place where all of the turmoil and the anxiety rests and abides. Likewise, the inside of a person is the place where solutions lie and where final outcomes of tragedy can be overcome. Just as the effects of being creative can sometimes drive one insane, the effects of being creative can sometimes cause one to have the greatest existence of all.

I have seen all of these points of light in different people that I have encountered from the poorest to the richest of my friends. I have seen friends who don't have much and are the happiest people in the world. Alternatively, I've seen people who have everything and are the loneliest, and saddest, and meanest people I have ever seen. Finding happiness is a hard thing to do when you are a creative type, but when you find it, happiness is a wonderful space to exist in. Simply stated, happiness is where your creativity and your peace can be in one place at the same time.

One of my greatest friends, who is a pastor, told me something that I shall always remember. He said that he told his congregation that he would rather have peace than joy any day, for peace overrides joy, because joy comes through things. While joy comes through having money and having friends, peace comes when all of those things don't cause you strife. They don't cause you pain. They don't cause you anxiety.

You have peace when you can just sit in a rocking chair, on any given porch around the world, and see in the distance nothing but purity of thought, with the clearest of mind and drink tea and eat chicken wings, without worrying about a thing. Ironically that would be my grandmother's favorite snack while watching her nightly television shows. That is peace, a synonym of happiness, and that is where I want to be.

My Grandmother's Faith

Give Me A Clean Heart

By
C. Michael Hawn

Give me a clean heart so I may serve you.
Lord, fix my heart so that I may be used by you.
For I'm not worthy of all these blessings.
Give me a clean heart and I'll follow you.
I'm not asking for the riches of the land.
I'm not asking for the proud to know my name.
Please give me, Lord, a clean heart,
that I may follow you.
Give me a clean heart, a clean heart
and I will follow you.
Sometimes I am up and sometimes I am down.
Sometimes I am almost level to the ground.
Please give me, Lord, a clean heart,
that I may follow you.
Give me a clean heart, a clean heart
and I will follow you.

Rodney Dean Boyden

Chapter Two: The Handshake

On Wednesday morning, October 21, 2015, I awakened to the realization that most of my day would be consumed with preparing for what promised to be one of the most interesting opportunities to ever come my way. Oh yes! This was indeed a special day, for I was going to meet one of the most important people of my lifetime and perform on stage for a national audience. Everything had to be perfect! From childhood, I was taught that success comes when preparation meets opportunity. I was definitely going to be prepared, because this was one of the greatest opportunities of my life. I had to be prepared, because the world would be watching.

Today's task was something that I had done many times before and I was prepared to perform on a moment's notice. But, never had I imagined that Terry Berkley would be the one to ask me to perform under these circumstances. When Terry was a little girl, her mother asked me to sew an Easter dress for her. She still has the dress to this day. Who would have thought that this little girl would be the catalyst for such a request?

Because of the type of event, my attire for the day had to be conservative and comfortable. I was sure of this fact, because I had laid out my garments and accessories on the night before. The brown pen-striped suit, gold and burgundy striped tie, white shirt with French cuffs, and my polished camel wing tip chocolate-toed lace-up shoes, were all ready to go. I got dressed and headed out of the house.

Within a few miles of the building, the roadblocks began, but, given the occasion, I knew that security was going to be extremely tight. Finally, I parked my car and approached event security, received my security clearance after emptying my pockets of the few possessions that I had brought with me. Once cleared through the security checkpoint, I passed through the rest of the secure zone without incident. Inside of the meeting area, there was more security and many excited people. I was ushered into a room filled with cameras, computers, and reporters who were ready to document the next moments in history.

It is widely known that my home state of West Virginia has a serious prescription drug overdose problem. Today's event had been organized to address this problem on a national platform and the two hundred of us who were invited to attend were ready for the beginning of the discussion.

My job was to perform a song. Not just any song, but one of the most difficult songs that anyone would ever be asked to sing — The National Anthem. In addition to knowing the words and tune, one must make sure that nerves and stage fright do not get in the way of a successful rendition. The Star-Spangled Banner must be delivered error free and without hesitation. The song can be either very easy to sing or, sadly, the most difficult to ever leave the mouth of the singer. Fortunately, I've sung this song many times before, so I was mentally prepared for the reality that the only sound in the room would be generated from my vocal chords vibrating throughout the atmosphere, probably over a large microphone system, and not shadowed by any music. On the occasion that this song is done a capella, without musical accompaniment, it makes for a much more stressful and difficult situation.

Show time was almost near and there I was standing behind the stage looking out upon the audience. Then, I was informed that, after my performance, I would be seated alongside state and city dignitaries, who had come to see the VIP of the event. As I looked toward where I was told my seat was located, I saw my name. Exactly the same as the names of the Governor, Senator, Mayor, and other important guests, my name was printed on a sheet of paper and attached to a chair, nearest the stage. I deeply appreciated this gesture, because it publicly displayed whose seat that would be on that very important day. Normally, a seating arrangement was not a huge deal to me at all, but on that day, IT WAS A BIG DEAL!!! Why? Well, because the particular piece of paper bearing my name came from one of the most important and famous houses in the world. It was stamped with the White House logo and placed there by the White House staff. I made a mental note to retrieve the paper at the end of the event in order to store it with my other memorable keepsakes.

Suddenly the room got quiet as the audience heard the announcer say, "ladies and gentlemen here to sing the Star-Spangled Banner is Mr. Rodney Dean Boyden." Now I need you to understand that after that announcement, the room got extremely loud again. There was the hustle and bustle of chairs and papers and coats and jackets and all of the things that people might have in their hands, shifting so that they could stand up for the singing of this patriotic song – The National Anthem.

I began walking towards the podium. The ten to fifteen feet seemed like I was walking a mile. However, during that 20 second walk, my mind was racing a million miles an hour, as I thought, "Oh my God!... Do I know the words?... What if I can't remember the song?... If I forget, what will happen then?" All of those scenarios, of what could go wrong, rushed to the forefront of my mind. In times like these, I don't automatically think about what can go right, but my mental tape usually repeats what could go wrong. This time, however, was a little different. In addition to my mind telling me how bad it would be for my career, if I messed this up, it also added how great this could be for me, if I did well. I know that I am not alone, for those are the thoughts that go through the minds of singers before an important performance such as this occasion.

Finally, as I neared the podium, the sound of moving chairs came to a screeching halt. Both of my feet landed right at the podium and there was no one there, but me, all by myself, standing straight, waiting for my heart to slow its rapid beating. I gauged my breathing and I knew that in between one of those heartbeats, I would begin to sing. After saying a little prayer and the One – one thousand, two – one thousand, three – one thousand of preparation began, I took a deep breath, and I realized how completely silent the room had become. It was as if no one was breathing. It was as if no one was moving. It was as if everyone had come to the conclusion that this moment must be respected. I began to sing:

> Oh, say can you see
> By the dawn's early light,
> What so proudly we hailed
> At the twilight's last gleaming?
> Whose broad stripes and bright stars
> Thru the perilous fight,
> O'er the ramparts we watched

Were so gallantly streaming?
And the rockets' red glare,
The bombs bursting in air,
Gave proof through the night
That our flag was still there.
Oh, say does that star-spangled banner yet wave,
O'er the land of the free and the home of the brave.

It was an amazing thing, because, once I started, there was no stopping and there was no room for mistakes. The words to this powerful anthem only come forth without pressure to those who really know them. Those who don't really know the words can become confused and start thinking that they have forgotten something. Oh My Goodness, OMG! God forbid, that a line be repeated or left out, which is something that has happened to some unsuspecting culprits at some point in time in the history of the world.

Today was not the day for mistakes and much to my great appreciation I made it through the song, without delay, without mistake, and welcomed a large round of applause for a few seconds after "the home of the brave." I walked off the stage in total gratitude for what I had just been blessed to experience. I was dazed by what had just happened. The two and a half to three minutes seemed like a process that took forever and I must say just one more time that I was grateful, in fact, very grateful that it was successfully over. I took my seat beside the Senator from the State of West Virginia and I enjoyed the rest of the program.

Now you must understand the gravity of this moment, because it is something that not many have the opportunity to experience. After the program ended, every moment became even more important, because I knew that in the next few seconds, I would touch and shake the hand of the sitting, President of the United States of America. The closer he came, the more I realized the gravity of that moment. The President was taller and leaner than I expected and when he stepped in front of me, my life came full circle. As I gazed into the eyes of the most powerful man in the free world, quickly I thought of my grandmother. Mamma had done all that was necessary in order to make this day possible. She had made sure that the circumstances surrounding my birth would not handicap my life's purpose. On this October day, three months shy of my fiftieth birthday, not only had I performed for the most powerful man in the free world, now I stood in front of him about to shake his hand.

The first African American President of the United States of America, President Barack Hussein Obama, was standing in front of me, reaching for my hand. He looked at me, shook my hand, and he said, "Thank you." I looked him in the eye, shook his hand and I said, "You're welcome, and we appreciate you." With that, the President continued down the line to speak to the rest of the people who were in the room. It was in that moment that I realized that a story must be told about how in the world I went from being adopted by my grandparents at birth to standing and holding the hand of the President of the United States of America.

Rodney Dean Boyden

If I Can Help Somebody

by
Alma Irene Bazel Androzzo

If I can help somebody as I pass along,
If I can cheer somebody with a word or a song,
If I can show somebody he is traveling wrong,
    Then my living shall not be in vain!

    Then my living shall not be in vain,
    Then my living shall not be in vain!
If I can help somebody as I pass along,
    Then my living shall not be in vain!

If I can do my duty as a Christian oft,
If I can bring back beauty to a world up wrought,
If I can spread love's message that the Master taught,
    Then my living shall not be in vain!

    Then my living shall not be in vain,
    Then my living shall not be in vain!
If I can help somebody as I pass along,
    Then my living shall not be in vain!

Chapter Three: Location of Validation

What makes me different than everyone else? What gives me the right to believe that I am special in any way? These are questions that I have pondered for as long as I have been alive. I concluded that the sum total of the creative abilities and talents that I was blessed with from birth have taken my mind down many paths and presented me with grand opportunities. However, it is that collection of emotional, psychological, social, and most importantly, religious underpinnings that my grandmother provided for me during my first twenty-seven years of life that have enabled me to lend value to society in a creatively unique way. My grandmother's faith in God and in me allowed her to validate me and nurture my talents, while raising me in a church-based, Christian, environment that left an indelible mark in my memory and in my heart.

Recently a conversation with a friend caused me to think of my youth in great detail. There were just a million instances where I was able to witness and feel a certain emotion and a certain feeling throughout my days as a youngster, while growing up with Mamma. You see, I grew up during the late 1960s and 70s, and one of the things that I liked so much about life was the one-on-one time that I had with her. Now when we talk about one-on-one time, you must understand my setting.

When my grandfather built our house, he put a chain link fence around our yard. The purpose of the chain link fence was to ensure that people did not just come into the yard. He would drive the cars into the driveway and shut the gate, but it was never locked. In those days, just shutting things was enough, but today, you can have all types of security alarms, dogs, cats, birds "quacking", horses "mooing", and people still will break in to your property. Back during that time though, a shut gate was enough to keep people away. Another purpose of the chain link fence was to keep our dogs in the yard. The fence did not cover the entire acreage that our house sat on, but the dogs were only impressed with the fencing nearest to them and did not try to get out of the yard in any other direction that I recall.

I mention the chain link fence, because it reminds me of the perimeters that can be around our insulated existences. For inside of our own little worlds, our protected spaces, where our mothers and fathers lived, and in my case where my grandmother and I resided, we spent a lot of alone time. I was insulated, more than not, by the love and care that she gave me. She was queen of my heart and I was her little king. I loved it and so did she.

The wonderful thing about being in our yard was that I could do all of the things that were creative while I was there. I loved it, because it was beautiful, it was very big, and impressive. Even today, when I return to Beckley, WV and ride by our old residence, I see the yard and I know that my footprints are pressed within the dirt, because I treaded on each part of that yard at some point in my life, either while playing with my dogs, walking around, or cutting the grass. I can still feel my spirit in the yard, even though our family doesn't own the house anymore.

Thinking back on those days of the chain link fence, I can picture its gate. The purpose of the gate was to let us out or to let us in to the yard. We could open the gate ourselves, someone could open the gate for us, we could close the gate, or someone could close the gate for us. The opening and closing of the gate to that yard is very symbolic to me and evokes a myriad of thoughts related to my childhood as well as to the larger world. Once I opened the gate and voluntarily went out into this world, I stepped outside of my point of validation. Inside of the gate, there was love. There were all of the things that were needed to pump me up and to let me know that I was a great kid, that I was a great person, and that I mattered in that house. But once I opened the gate myself and closed it myself, I voluntarily stepped my foot out into the world in which genuine acceptance no longer existed. I found out that people don't always think that you are as special as your mother thought that you were. They don't see the same qualities in you. They don't witness the same special traits that you have that she found to be so cute and so wonderful. They think that you are just another person.

When I was a little boy, I was a "small" boy. When I was growing up everybody was larger than me in my neighborhood. Now, I wasn't Benjamin Button, but I was not Hulk Hogan. I was not muscular. In fact, I was short and lanky. I was a thin, very bright, little yellow child, with an Afro and big teeth. To give you a better perspective, in the tenth grade, I only weighed a hundred and forty-five pounds, and 145 in the 10th grade was very little, by the standards of the football players and some of the other friends that I had in the same grade.

I was thin and I was little, because I had not come into myself at that point. Nevertheless, I enjoyed playing what we called "sandlot" football. Sandlot football, for those of you who don't know, is when you go out among your friends and just start playing an impromptu game of football in the grass. That means in any field of grass that was large enough to where we could run at full speed and not run into something, such as a building or a car, it was open game for that to be the place where we were going to play football. And we loved playing football.

Now the problem was that I was little. Everyone knew that I was very fast, but I didn't necessarily have all the skills at that point to be a football player and surely not a basketball player. The sight of me playing basketball is comedy at its best. The thing about it is that when you're little, the other kids treat you a certain way. They do certain things to you. They knock you around, just because you're little, just because they're bigger than you, and just because they can easily push you around on the field or the court. There you are, in that life, outside of your comfort zone, and your grandma can't do anything about it. Those kids can do whatever they want to do. They can hit you over the head and crack your baseball cap. They can throw you over hills in the snow and make you cry like a little baby. They can beat you up and sock you in the nose and you go home all bloody. They can trip you and make you fall with your schoolbooks. They can do all types of things, but the one thing about it is that how you handle being treated that way depends on the type of person that you are on the inside.

The thing that I loved so much about the validation that I got from my Mamma was that I knew, beyond a shadow of a doubt, that even in the midst of my minuscule infirmities, the validation that I got from home allowed me to keep on trying. It allowed me to keep on pushing. It allowed me to keep on going. It allowed me to keep on running to see what the end would be, because I did not necessarily need the validation of those people. Even in my lack of developed skills, I kept on moving. I kept on doing. I kept on creating in my own space. You see sometimes you don't need validation in one area, because you are validating yourself in another area.

One pastor said, "You need to encourage yourself." Sometimes you need to look in the mirror and say, "you are good." No matter what they say," you say, "you are good." God created you and He said, "you are good", if you are good, you're good.

I know so many football players that went to my high school who were grand and wonderful, but now, life has come down on them and the grandeur of the high school experience has waned. When I look on the other side, I remember my high school years and the unpopularity of not being muscular and big. Now, the tables have turned and I am even more grateful for the validation that Mamma gave me, which enabled me to excel in my own right. What a wonderful thing to be able to have control of my mental gate now. Since we don't own the house anymore, I go to that chain link fence in my mind and I look around. In my mind's eye, I look at the grass and I think of all the times that I was able to just go back home and shut that gate behind me and just pull that little metal latch knowing that back there was all the validation that I ever really needed.

Sometimes, we do too much worrying about things that really don't matter. We worry about what people think and about what they say, when all that we need to understand is that God is all that we need. For me, knowledge of God initially came through my grandmother. Mamma showed me a level of validation that has lasted me to this very day, because even in my adult life, people still like to talk about me. Sometimes folk don't even know me, and just make up stuff, but I am not discouraged, because I have been created by the greatest of all. This validation, for me, is found at the foot of the cross where Jesus was hung and died. Where His blood dripped down to the hard floor of the bare rock on the hill called Calvary. That is where your validation should lie. I know it sounds a little deep and maybe even a little cliché, but we must stop looking for it in the wrong location. I ask you right now to go inside of the chain link fence of your soul, shut the gate behind you, stand up straight and say I've got validation. I am in a state of validation. Today, I give validation in the Name of Jesus. And He gives validation to you today.

Rodney Dean Boyden

Higher Ground

by
Johnson Oatman, Jr.

"I'm pressing on the upward way;
New heights I'm gaining everyday;
Still praying as I'm onward bound;
Lord plant my feet on higher ground."

Lord, lift me up and let me stand;
By faith, on Heaven's tableland;
A higher plane than I have found;
Lord, plant my feet on higher ground.

My heart has no desire to stay
Where doubts arise and fears dismay;
Though some may dwell where those abound,
My prayer, my aim, is higher ground.

I want to live above the world,
Though Satan's darts at me are hurled;
For faith has caught the joyful sound,
The song of saints on higher ground.

I want to scale the utmost height
And catch a gleam of glory bright;
But still I'll pray till heav'n I've found,
"Lord, plant my feet on higher ground."

Chapter Four:
My Safety Net

I have always had a fascination with bridges, as they symbolize hope, progress, connections, and stability. There have been battles fought on, over, and around bridges for centuries. One is the Battle of Milvian Bridge, which embodies each of those symbolizations. According to Christian history, the battle took place about 1704 years ago between Roman Emperors Constantine I and Maxentius in AD 312 or 313. Constantine was a pagan monotheist, devoted to the sun god, Sol Invictus, meaning the unconquered sun. Before the Milvian Bridge battle, he and his army saw a cross of light in the sky with words in Greek, that when translated in Latin, meant, "In this sign conquer." That night, Constantine had a dream in which Christ told him to use the sign of the cross against his enemies. He obeyed and had a Cross "painted" on the shields of each of his soldiers. When they won the battle, Constantine attributed the victory to the God of the Christians and became a Christian himself. In AD 315, the Arch of Constantine was erected in Rome to commemorate Constantine's victory.

When I think of this battle, it reminds me of the New River Gorge Bridge that opened in Fayetteville, West Virginia in 1978 when I was 11 years old. It was constructed on a single-span steel arch 3,030 feet long and 875 feet high. The arch, being one of the strongest structural shapes in architecture, is a curved structure that converts the downward force of its own weight and any weight pressing down on top of it will be transferred into an outward force along its sides and base. The arch is constructed of individual building blocks that can support a certain amount of weight standing alone.

For many years, the New River Gorge Bridge was the longest of its kind in the world. Now, it is the third longest. It takes a unique mind to understand this structure and it took special people with unique characteristics and expertise to assemble it. Before the first piece of approach span steel could be erected, stories were spreading among highway workers about the potential employment of Mohawk Indians, known for their ability to walk the "high steel" of New York City skyscrapers. Builders of tall projects have to be comfortable with working while being suspended from cables or standing on platforms that are thousands of feet above the earth's surface. I cannot resist thinking of the connection that the Mohawk Indians must have had with the earth. It can be attributed to their comfort and spiritual connection to this land hundreds of years before the Nina, the Pinta, and the Santa Maria ever touched ground on the shores of the Caribbean islands. These islands are just a hop, skip, and a big jump from the mainland of North America. Out of all the information that surrounded this bridge, the type of worker that was needed is something that I have never forgotten.

Workers must at all times pay close attention to their surroundings or their equilibrium and ability to stand up straight can be greatly impaired. No matter how brave, how strong, or how skilled workers are, accidents can and do occur during the construction process. When in the building process, there had to be preparation for the possibility of accidents that would require something in place to break the fall and catch the workers. That something came in the form of a strong safety net that spanned the entire area under the bridge. It was designed to catch or break the fall of workers to ensure that no one got hurt and fell to their death.

It is fascinating to think that just as the New River Gorge Bridge was constructed on a spectacular arch for support, the safety net was still needed to protect the workers from falling. It reminds me that life's bridges take us from one place to the next dependent upon our actions and reactions to the circumstances that occur on our paths. My grandmother was my arch and my safety net all wrapped up in one neat package from the beginning of my life until I was twenty-seven years old.

I liken my grandmother's faith to a Roman arch, because her faith has been the strong support that has allowed me to progress to my present place in life. My grandmother was able to accomplish this task as she provided me with an environment that enabled the development of the building blocks for what would prove to be my life's staircase. Mamma understood and noticed in small ways that I was working very hard to perfect all of my gifts and she would look at me and say, "you can do it." She just let me go and learn in my own time, not with pressure, but with that oh so gentle push to succeed. I was able to take the time to put my mind on each skill and to understand the problem solving components that were needed in order to advance in each area. She allowed me to work at my own pace and she loved me unconditionally during those years of this process. Her love was consistent when I bumped my head and was bleeding and needed stitches, when my stomach was hurting from shrimp poisoning, when I wrecked a car, or when I did not do well in school. For that matter, she would walk to the school, if there were a problem, which I recall on several occasions. She loved me in spite of the down times. She just loved me and each of those times strengthened a block in my inner arch. I know this fact, because I can recall the simple things that she did to show over and over again the work that she put in that contributed to the skill set that I have today. Sometimes I was going down on one side of the arch and at other times I was headed up the other side in my attempts to learn and somehow as only grandmothers can do, Mamma could see my progress even when I could not and she kept right on loving me through the struggles.

These struggles were exacerbated during my teen years as I was torn between two loves. I, at times, abandoned Mamma when I fell for one of the smartest and most popular girls in town. For the first time something pulled me away from her and it was painful for both of us. For Mamma, the pain was immediate, but for me it came years later after I reflected on those times. Out of the two loves, Mamma's love was the only love not laced in conditions. This showed in her actions when even in her disappointment, she wiped my tears when my young love dissipated.

Mamma was there to make sure that even when I fell down, everything I needed was there when I stood up again. Because of this consistent love and care, even as a little child, I had inside of me a mandate to be the best and to keep growing and learning. I knew that I was suspended from my favorite arch and I was protected by my ever present safety net, all in one endeared grandmother.

I must confess that when my son was growing up and I went to visit him and his mother, it seemed early on that all he wanted was to play video games. When he saw me, I must have looked like a big Nintendo game cartridge, because it was the first thing out of his little mouth. It never failed, "Can you buy me a game"? He said. Looking back on those days, I always felt like that was all he ever wanted from me. Now, after years of living and experiencing the family dynamic, I know that, from the people you love and the people that are to be the arches and safety nets in your life, the pieces of the human construction process require things like material, laborers, and skill. When translated it simply means to provide all of the things kids need to grow in life, from that video game all the way to that first car. It wasn't that my son wanted things from me, but he had the same need from me that I needed from my grandmother. It was unconditional love and expectation!

I remember the shopping trips to G.C. Murphy, when I was a child, and how it seemed that all I had to do was literally snap my tiny fingers and toys would appear. If I said I needed a new band instrument, it was there. If I needed some new clothes, they were there. If I needed a new car, she tried to make it happen. Whatever I needed, she made sure that I had it as soon as possible. She loved me and, unlike myself who was young with a 4-year old son, she had years of understanding, from raising her own two children. She knew what an arch did, but I didn't! I had not made the connection, because I, myself, was still in "Receive mode." I didn't have any worries, because, when I walked around and I looked around, I was able to just be aware of the world, knowing that whatever I needed, I had somebody who was able to make it happen in my world.

As a boy and later as a young man, I depended on that consistency that she had created and I was so grateful to know that I had a safety net. Now, as a mature adult, I look back and know that I could have done much better in terms of my choices, my decision-making, and my chosen paths. I know that, even though I was working hard to perfect my craft, rescuing me was not always good for me. I admit that sometimes, the safety net did not let me fall as far as I needed to fall in order to get the point of the lesson that needed to be learned in certain situations. Nevertheless, Mamma's love and her nurturing nature imprinted my life in a profound way.

Just as the safety net allowed the bridge workers to complete the project with a certain sense of protection, my safety net allowed me to grow up with that same protected feeling. The years that we were together allowed me the space and flexibility to matriculate and learn, while creating enough talent blocks, so that when the net was taken away, the arch that she was and the arch that she had created in me could stand — alone. When Mamma left, it would be my arch that would have to stand the test. It was me against the world. The minute that she died, I had to be prepared to go through that experience without killing myself. The minute that she died my immediate family made me realize as we sat at Mamma's dining room table reading her will, that in no uncertain terms you are about to stand up and be a man, because your safety net, my friend, is gone and we are NOT its replacements! Much to their credit, they have kept their word! The one person in this world that I knew was for me, was gone!

I am so grateful to tell you that the building blocks of the arch that Mamma nurtured were strong enough to hold up the roads of my life. Not without mistakes and trials, but I continue to stand. While Mamma lived, she was my bridge and safety net and God was her arch as she had been mine. Upon her death, her faith became my faith and her God became my God.

I am grateful to have been her adopted son and to have been loved by her. Now I stand and look to God, who is the author and finisher of my faith, just as He was the author and finisher of my grandmother's faith. I am thankful for each new opportunity that God is giving me. Whichever of my talents are being highlighted, I am thankful for each chance to showcase my inner arch. I know that I have got a God who is strong and I also know that the life that he has set forth for me will, at times, test the strength of my inner structural integrity. Thanks to God and to Mamma, I have that ability that undergirds the road of my life. I know that it will hold me up, no matter what may come my way, because I am strong, I am tough, and I can take a licking and keep on ticking. My grandmother showed me that no matter what, I can make it. I can cross the mountain. I can cross the road. I can. I will, because of God working in my life. Thank you God for giving her to me, because now, I can see to the other side. Without fear and without trembling, I can stand up tall and say, "Yes, I am an arch and I've got an arch on the inside that resounds — you are strong enough to take the pressure."

My Grandmother's Faith

My Hope is Built on Nothing Less

by
Edward Mote

My hope is built on nothing less
Than Jesus' blood and righteousness;
I dare not trust the sweetest frame,
But wholly lean on Jesus' name.
On Christ, the solid Rock, I stand;
All other ground is sinking sand.

When darkness veils His lovely face,
I rest on His unchanging grace;
In every high and stormy gale
My anchor holds within the veil.
On Christ, the solid Rock, I stand;
All other ground is sinking sand.

His oath, His covenant, and blood
Support me in the whelming flood;
When every earthly prop gives way,
He then is all my Hope and Stay.
On Christ, the solid Rock, I stand;
All other ground is sinking sand.

When He shall come with trumpet sound,
Oh, may I then in Him be found,
Clothed in His righteousness alone,
Faultless to stand before the throne!
On Christ, the solid Rock, I stand;
All other ground is sinking sand.

Rodney Dean Boyden

Chapter Five:
The Day I Walked Away

The irony of life is amazing to me. Andy Warhol is credited with saying, "people sometimes say the way things happen in the movies is unreal, but actually, it's the way things happen to you in real life that's unreal." I could not agree more with that utterance. On Mother's Day 2016, I was back home in West Virginia, preparing to pen this very emotional chapter, because I needed to be in close proximity to where the actual events took place. After church, I went to visit the grave-site of my good friend, Evangelist Angela M. Charlton-Coston (Angie or Ang). In 2007, at only thirty-nine years of age, Ang passed away of lung cancer. She had never smoked a day in her life, but her father was a smoker. Angie was a really special person and a good friend, whom I really loved a lot. Mother's Day was the first time that I had an opportunity to visit her grave and my emotions were reaching into the dirt to touch my friend's spirit again.

Seated on a cement bench at the head of her grave, I stared across at the words etched in the metal footstone. She is buried beside her father in the place where her mother would have been buried under normal circumstances. Since Angie died before her mother, the plot became hers. I speak of ANG now; because of the role she played in the story that I am about to tell.

I am recalling this story at Angie's grave; because hers was the voice that uttered the most dreaded words to me so many years ago. In December of 1993, I entered a talent show that was being held at a hotel in the heart of Charleston, West Virginia. I loved talent shows. One reason was because I had a boatload of confidence and I usually felt that I was going to win. Another reason was because the cash prizes ranged from $300 to $3000, which in 1985 through the 1990s was a lot of money.

On this particular evening, I was backstage waiting for my name to be called, when my Motorola DynaTAC cell phone rang. A huge phone, by today's standards, the DynaTAC looked like something off of Star Trek. Back then though; it was a big deal to own one. I remember it as if it was yesterday. I even remember the clothes that I was wearing when the phone rang. I answered the phone to hear Angie's voice on the other end. She asked where I was and when I responded that I was at a talent show at the hotel, then she asked if I was alone. Now anybody who's old enough, knows this loaded question is usually followed by a more powerful statement or action. However, I was so busy preparing for the show that the peculiar nature of her questions, as well as her corresponding statements, were lost on me. She replied that she was on her way up there. I told her to hurry, because I was about to go on stage. A short while later, she came through the door.

Angie always wore a smile and had a cheerful persona. Our time spent together was filled with laughing and joking. Positive dialogue was our norm. That day, however, Ang's face was flushed with redness and she was disheveled. When she looked me in the eye, even before her mouth started moving, I knew that something had gone terribly wrong. Her next words changed my life forever. "Your grandmother has died."

As soon as Ang's words formed the auditory signal that entered my ear canals, their vibrations registered in my brain. My universe stopped revolving and all of its stars went out. The one person on earth, who loved me unconditionally, was dead. I was mortified!!! My mind and my body went numb. From that point on, I could not feel. I could not hear. I could not touch. I could not taste. Nothing was the same as prior to hearing those words. I remember clearly going into the restroom and losing all of the confidence and composure that I had mustered for the stage. I was overtaken by complete and utter sadness, grief, loneliness, and pure despair. After getting myself back to some semblance of togetherness, I called Jack, my manager at the time, and asked him to travel with me to my hometown, which was about 55 miles away. The short distance of 55 miles seemed like 1200 miles in the car.

Several years earlier, Mamma had been diagnosed with cancer, specifically multiple myeloma, which caused her to be bedridden for many years. While discussing long-term care, she made it very clear that she never wanted to go into a nursing home. Her words, were not merely a fleeting sentiment, but formed a clear and ever present directive to everyone involved. Mamma said, "I do not want to go to a nursing home" and we heard her loud and clear. When she was no longer able to take care of herself, we arranged for Ms. J.J. Johnson (JJ), a wonderful home health aide, to join our family as Mamma's full-time, in-home caretaker. JJ was a godsend, which assisted in taking care of Mamma day in and day out. Her presence in our home made everything much easier on a daily basis. Keeping Mamma as comfortable as possible was JJ's priority.

When I arrived at the funeral home, Mamma was lying on a gurney under a sheet. Mamma, the person whom I considered to be the love of my life, lay silent, empty, and motionless. To this day, I know that it was nobody, but the Almighty God, who took over every function of my entire being and enabled me to stand. How I actually laid eyes on my Mamma, in that position, in that situation, and was able to walk out of the room on my own two feet, is still a mystery to me.

When I left the funeral home, Jack drove me home. Up until that point, one of the most difficult things that I have ever experienced was the day we drove back into the driveway, knowing that Mamma was not there. I was heart broken and crushed, to say the least.

Mamma was not there, but of course neighbors, friends, and family, who lived in the city had gathered at the house by this time. They witnessed my arrival and each person knew that this was going to be an overwhelming experience for me to deal with at this point in my life. When I walked into the house, the lights seemed dimmer. When I walked into the house, the feeling of love seemed absent from the atmosphere. When I walked into the house, the air seemed as if it had been sucked out of the entire space. Once filled with love and warmth, now, the house was only a shell of its former self. Only a shell, because it no longer housed the very soul and very presence of the one I loved. I walked into the house and instead of seeing Mamma and feeling love, I merely saw nouns. Yes, nouns, which are people, places, and things. My world lost all verbs and adjectives; since Mamma was gone, it contained just a bunch of nouns.

For the next few days, the usual funeral preparation ensued and all of the regular preparatory activities took place. Everything was brought to our home. There was food. There was drink. There was dessert. The funeral director visited the house to ask the normal questions. We later went to the funeral home where my birth mother and uncle allowed me to pick out the casket. I was in a state of shock and merely going through the motions in a catatonic state of disbelief, however I did what I had to do in this trying time. The idea of me picking out a painted box, lined with fabric and pillows that would house the body of my Mamma was surreal, but we made sure that Mamma was eulogized in a manner that would have made her proud.

It amazes me how families choose things for the dead that the dead themselves aren't able to appreciate. Obviously, it is for our own sanity that we purchase items such as self-sealing caskets and cement vaults that supposedly; doesn't allow moisture and water into the chamber. Whether or not these expensive products actually keep moisture and water out is something that the living is never able to corroborate. However, purchasing these items provides the self-assuredness that as a last and final action, the family gave the deceased a decent burial.

After I chose the casket, there was what most would call the family viewing. It was the day that we saw Mamma for the first time in her final clothing, in her final peaceful position, and in her final visual on earth. We entered the back of the room and I sat down to just take in the aura and smell of the room and experience the silence. I needed to take all of this moment-by-moment, because moving too quickly might have been disruptive to my very sanity. I asked my mother and my uncle to go ahead along with the rest of the family and have their moments. For years, there had been nobody in the house, but Mamma and me, together alone, experiencing space as a team. This was the day when I would walk up and see my partner in crime, my team member, my ride or die chick, my friend, my one and only, my all-in-all, laying there with nothing to say, with no purpose, with no action, with nothing. I would accept the reality that she was no longer there when I was standing in front of her. I needed to say my final goodbye to Mamma alone and I was not going to do that in the presence of others. I had to do this all by myself.

Sitting there in the funeral home, I smiled as I recalled various conversations Mamma and I had during some of her hospital stays. Always, when I told her that I loved her more than anything, her grayish, hazel eyes would twinkle as she looked into my eyes. Each time, following those tender moments, we always laughed. Yes, me telling Mamma that I loved her made her laugh, but she was also laughing, because of something else that I often added to that statement. I would say to her, "Mamma, you know that I love you...but when you die, I want you to stay dead..., because if you come back to help me, or ever let me see you again, I will kill myself running from you." Oh, did my saying those words tickle her! Mamma would laugh and laugh, but as she laughed, I thought to myself, "she thinks I'm joking, but I'm serious!"

Over the years, those thoughts of Mamma have brought me much laughter. Remembering those times with her are the very recollections that keep me going. To this day, the mental images of Mamma smiling at me and knowing that she was looking at me through pain, knowing that she was looking at me through hurt, and knowing that she was looking at me through the uncertainty of her near future, still lift my spirits high.

After the rest of the family had gone, I approached her casket. Mamma had requested to be dressed in the mauve colored, soft sheer, silk dress that she had worn for my uncle's wedding, during happier times. Now, please understand that I do not like the color mauve. In fact, mauve is my least favorite color in the entire world. However, Mamma loved the color, so on that day, so did I. With her hair freshly curled, make-up flawlessly done, glasses positioned perfectly, and white gloves on her dainty hands, Mamma looked like her normal beautiful self.

Before I continue, let me make something else perfectly clear. I am afraid of dead people. So, what I did next with Mamma was very uncharacteristic of me. Nonetheless, I needed to do that one final thing. Standing beside her casket, I lifted one of her white-gloved hands and put my hand in between her hands. In order to picture this, envision Mamma's right hand on her stomach, my right hand on top of it, her left hand on top of that, and my left hand on top of hers. I sandwiched her hands in mine, so that I could once again feel her holding my hands. Even though there was no feeling, there was no warmth, there was no response from her, and still I stood there for approximately one and a half hours, talking to Mamma. I let her know, in every way, with every word, and with every phrase that I could come up with, how much I absolutely loved her and how much I was going to miss her.

As I stood there rambling on and pleading for things that I did not want, I said some really silly things. I said, "Mamma, if you love me, would you just show me a sign?" "Mamma, just move a little bit, so that I know that you care." "Mamma, if you would just let me have a sign that you know that I'm here, I would feel so much better." After about an hour and a half of "Mamma this" and "Mamma that," I had gotten it all out. I had cried my last tears, for the moment. I had offered all of my verbal accolades, yet Mamma continued to just lay there in silence. In that moment, I came back to myself and realized my hands were sandwiched between the hands of a dead person. Yes, it was Mamma, but Mamma was dead.

Suddenly, a big smile came upon my face and I began to laugh and laugh and laugh, but when I started laughing, I started shaking, so now both me and the casket and Mamma are moving!!!!!!!! MOOOOVVIINNNGGGG!!!!!!!!!! All of the crazy things that I had just told her went straight out the window! In that moment, I realized that if Mamma would have moved a finger on her own, if she would have tweaked, if she would have even so much as flinched any part of her hand or body, or if a door had slammed or anything in that room had toppled over, I would have killed myself trying to get out of there. Whether through one of the walls to my left, to my right, or maybe even straight-ahead knocking her out the casket and me killing myself, Rodney would have been rapidly leaving the building. This was as funny to me as it possibly could get, because Mamma and I had gotten one last hearty laugh as her casket came to a standstill. With that interlude of needed humor, I returned to the real world and continued the burial process.

Mamma died on December 2, 1993. December is usually cold and a very snowy time of year in West Virginia, and the day of the funeral seemed much colder then normal. The long green trench coat and hat that I wore reminded me of all of the ways that Mamma had provided for me over the years. During the course of that day, a lifetime of memories flooded my mind. I remembered that Mamma always made sure that I had the nicest clothing. I had coats, hats, scarves, gloves, socks, shoes, jackets, and there was even one little thing that she got me, which was called a dickey. A dickey was a turtleneck without the full body of the garment. It was also called a mock turtleneck in that it could be worn under a shirt to protect the neck from the elements. Thanks to Mamma, I had them in all colors. The trench coat that I wore would cover my body that day, but it could not, and it would not shield me from the reality that I was about to witness. That day was to be Mamma's last day above the ground.

As I walked into the church in front of all of Mamma's friends, in front of all of my friends, in front of all of my family members, and my birth mother and her brother, I began the process of leaving Mamma for the last time. This was a heavy and strange experience for me. I felt as if I did not have the power to control anything. The very heart of my existence was lying in a casket and any sense that I had ever had of being rooted in the world, was diminished. I felt lost, helpless, robbed, and all alone. Mamma, my precious love, the only person who ever understood me, and who loved me unconditionally, was dead. Upon reaching the front of the church, I approached Mamma's open casket for the last time and slipped a letter inside that I had written to her and a picture of my son, Chris. Dazed and despondent, I sat as the funeral proceeded.

At the appointed time I sang, "If You Ask Him," by Richard Alan Henderson and Nezela W. Kirtz.

If You Ask Him

> He'll lift you up if you ask Him,
> He'll show you the way.
> He'll fill your cup if you ask Him,
> He'll brighten up your day.
> He'll hold your hand if you ask Him,
> He'll give you strength anew.
> He'll un-der-stand if you ask Him,
> He'll keep your secrets, too.
> He'll com-fort you if you ask Him,
> He'll keep you thru the night.
> He'll stay with you if you ask Him,
> He'll make things all right.
> He'll calm your fears if you ask Him,
> He'll give you peace of mind.
> He'll dry your tears if you ask Him,
> He'll give you joy divine

Over the 27 years that we were together, I had attended many funerals with Mamma and we had gone to the cemetery many times, as she said farewell to her friends, family members, and fellow church members. Our family had probably one of the largest headstones in the cemetery, if not the largest, with the word BOYDEN written on it. Upon driving into the cemetery, everyone knew without a doubt where our family was buried. It was the place that my grandfather was buried and where all of his brothers and sisters that had bought a burial plot took their final rest. Those who rested there already were waiting on Mamma's arrival, into this place of silence, into this place where once left they were never being moved again.

It was cold. Real cold. I got out of the car and walked over to her grave. The pallbearers had placed her casket in her last and final spot to be lowered into the cold ground, where her body would rest for eternity. I heard the faint words, "ashes to ashes," "dust to dust." The cold wind blew across my face as small hard tears ran down my cheek. I knew that soon the undertaker's words would follow, "the family may return to the cars for the repast". I became frozen in time.

A large part of me died that day. Completely numb, I could not tell if I was still alive. I asked myself questions even today as I pen these lines, "Did I walk away?" or "Am I still there?" "Is my heart still there?" "Is my soul still there?" "Is the very thing that makes me a human being still there, in that place with Mamma?" To a great extent, the answer is yes. A portion of me is stuck way back there with Mamma. The four seasons

— winter, spring, summer and fall, all come and go each year to find me still there, with Mamma. Figuratively, I am standing there in that spot, afraid to leave her, not wanting to leave her, needing to be there with her, because she was always there with me.

My body did walk away. It went to the church to find people laughing, enjoying food, and enjoying the time with family and friends. I remember sitting among them thinking, how can they smile? How can they laugh? How can there be a sound of jubilance in this room, at this moment, and at this time? It did not dawn on me until later that even though that was my time of mourning, there had been many days prior that I did the same thing following the funerals of others. I went to the church, ate food, drank soda, and moved on with my day, not knowing how it really felt. But today was my turn. It was my turn to not appreciate the sound of happiness, for it was not a happy day. It was the saddest day of my entire life. It was the day that I walked away.

As I complete this cathartic chapter, I realize that my body walked away, but my soul stayed at Mamma's grave, and my heart still resides there also. I understand that, because I did not give this life to myself and the length of its days do not lie within my control; crucial questions must be asked and answered. How do I live on? How do I walk around? How do I continue without Mamma? And the answer is... The only answer is --- God. God is the reason that I can continue, because without God I could, literally, do nothing. Without Him I would fail, Without Him my life would be completely rugged, like a ship without a sail. I love you Mamma. I'm still there with you. I know now that I didn't walk away. I am with you. Each time I visit your gravesite, I step back into a faded hologram of a 27-year old me in that green trench coat and hat that never left your side.

Rodney Dean Boyden

"Without God, I Could Do Nothing"

by
B. Brown

Without God, I Could Do Nothing
Yes,
Without God, I could do nothing, Oh Lord
Without God, You know all my life would fail
Without God, my life would be rugged, Oh Lord,
Yes, like a ship
Without a sail, without a sail

Without a doubt, he is my Savior,
Yes, my strength, along, along life's waves
Yes, in deep waters, my God, he is my anchor
Lord, & through faith he'll keep me always

I'm leanin and dependin on Jesus
And I'm trustin in him everyday
I'm waitin, I'm just waitin for my for my Savior
Because one of these old days he gonna dry all my tears away.

Chapter Six: Mind Regulator

My grandfather's love for cars drove him to own some really awesome automobiles. I learned to appreciate cool cars by watching him. Daddy's cars were shiny, beautiful, and wonderful. Sometimes, I would sit in the driveway and just stare at them, while at other times I swung on the swing in our yard and imagined myself driving. I was in awe of those magnificent machines and I can still see the white Deuce and a Quarter white-walled tires and glistening wheels in my mind. These tires were special, because they were made with a 2" white stripe and another ¼ inch stripe outside of it making for a look that was unmatched in luxury.

When I was old enough to drive and got my own cars, I always kept them clean and polished. I can still hear Mamma hollering out of the window on Saturday mornings, saying "Stop Using My Kitchen Towels To Wash The Car, Rodney!" I believe she told me that for 10 years, while continuing to replace the kitchen towels that I kept on using for the cars.

While thinking about all of the automobiles that we owned growing up, there is one that stands out in my memory, because it was one that I had just destroyed weeks earlier. This accident was a result of me at 16 years of age not knowing the effects of driving tired. I fell asleep while driving and wrecked my grandfather's last car on the Tennessee — Virginia state line. It was there that the 1978 Lincoln Continental Black Diamond Edition and I became acquainted with a large tree in the middle of the highway median at approximately 12:30 a.m. one night. I must say that I have never forgotten that car and it haunts my dreams at times to this day. Its replacement was a blue and gold 1978 Mercury Cougar, which had been given to us by my elegant Aunt Stella, my grandfather's youngest sister. She heard through the family grapevine that I needed a car, so when she and her husband, Uncle Robert decided to buy a new one, they gave us the Cougar.

The Cougar was a luxury edition with blue tweed seats and gold seat belts, and it had a blue and gold leather patch on the back of the trunk. To add to the Cougar's awesomeness, I added white wall tires and gold Craig rims. Oh, and that is not all. I attached a hood ornament of a silver woman with gold acrylic wings that lit up, along with lights over the wheels, so that at night the rims would shine and everyone could see Rodney coming. Little did I know that twenty years later lights over wheels would become a popular car decoration. Those were the days when I had the wonderful opportunity of sitting in our driveway and coming up with amazing concoctions that people still talk about to this day. Clearly, I was ahead of my time.

The Cougar was indeed a beautiful car, but there was one thing about it that I always found perplexing. As beautiful as the car was, and as wonderful as I had fixed it up to be, the Cougar had a big problem with its voltage regulator.

Now, the voltage regulator is a device that maintains the proper spark levels in a car's alternator. On the Cougar, it was located on the inner part of the hood over the fender well. When the voltage regulator malfunctioned, the alternator overcharged the electrical system and caused many of the car's components to fail.

This problem was perplexing to me, because in my mind, it was not supposed to exist in such a beautiful car. You see, I was focused on the car's physical beauty and how marvelously, as the young folk say, "I had tricked it out." I could not understand why this 'mean driving machine' was not running properly.

The reality was that when the voltage regulator went bad, the whole system of the car went topsy-turvy. This simply means that the car would not run. Interestingly enough, the voltage regulator was not an expensive part, but it was crucial to the Cougar's functionality and shut my beautiful car down. Day after day, my Cougar sat there in the yard, looking beautiful with its luxury package, hood ornament with wings, and lights over the wheels, but would not move. Without a voltage regulator, it was no longer worth a dime, but it sure did look good.

As we turn our attention away from engine regulation, let's think about the concept of mind regulation. Just as the voltage regulator regulates a car, our minds regulate our thoughts, words, actions and deeds. The difference between the human mind and a car engine is that the mind functions as an infinite open-ended thought process that is the result of brain activities, which have a conscious as well as a subconscious side.

Now, let's make a distinction here between the human mind and the brain. The brain is the central processing unit of the body that plays a key role in translating the content of the mind, including our thoughts, feelings, attitudes, beliefs, memories, and imagination. Interestingly enough, just as with the car engine, the mind must be regulated; this is necessary to set our parameters for the things that should and should not be said, as well as those that should and should not be done.

People use different terms to describe the thing, process, or person that helps to regulate the mind. Some people call it scruples. Some people call it morals. Some people call it a father figure. Some people call it a mentor. I believe that regardless of the form it takes, regulation of the mind simply means to give it direction, purpose, and a familiar point to which it can turn, when stabilization is necessary. It is necessary at all times, but especially when one has stepped over the side of possibility onto the slippery side of danger.

Everyone's mind needs regulating at some point in his or her life, but not everybody has his or her own mind regulator. In fact, I did not have a mind regulator until I was nearly thirty years old. When I was growing up, I noticed mind regulators in my friends' homes where fathers were present; however, my father was not present and my grandfather was not in our home on a regular basis. So, as a result, my mind was not really regulated by a voice that was strong enough to overpower my own creative thought process.

When a young boy is left to his own devices, without a man around, it opens up a cadre of possibilities, because there is no one to tell him what to do. This can create a dangerous situation, because the boy will come up with all types of reasons to not follow directions. Daddy was loved and revered in our community and in our home. He took care of everything. He sent money. He came home every few months and then he left again. This meant that I was at home, with Mamma, to be loved and cuddled and held, until sometimes I felt like she loved and cuddled and held me to death. Well, not to death, but to my detriment, because there was no mind regulation.

The only mind regulation that I received while growing up at home was the mind regulation that I allowed because of my love for Mamma. I say that I allowed a certain amount of mind regulation, because I was a little 14-year old boy being raised by a 67-year old lady and I felt so special. I allowed her to regulate me. This meant that I had my own parameters, but I really didn't have a wall to hit that would indicate when I had gone too far.

Sometimes my birth mother came over and when I did something crazy, she said, "Rodney, you're going to let a wheel run off." That was interesting, because when she said that, I knew that it could have meant a myriad of things like, I was about to go off of the deep end, what I was doing was out of line, I had gone a little too far, I said a little too much, or I was doing a little too much. That was pretty much the extent of my childhood mind regulation and that is what I call not having a mind regulator.

In 1996, I met the man who would become my mind regulator. We were from the same state and although, prior to that time, I had never met him in person, I had been watching him from a distance for years. I had seen him often in passing on the West Virginia highways and being a car guy, I took special note of the red Lincoln Continental with a white top that he drove. When I saw the red and white car pass by, I would say, "Yeah, there he is. He's on his way," because he was always on his way somewhere and usually I was on my way somewhere too.

At around the age of thirty, I had an opportunity to spend time talking with him. I knew immediately that those conversations would change my life and there was something that I was going to get from this brother that I had never gotten from a man in all of my life. It was mind regulation. For you see, a mind regulator is a person who has the ability, through their words and through their actions, to make you think about where you're putting your power and how you are using your power.

Soon I was working with him and our discussions continued. Sometimes he talked and at other times, I talked as we discussed things on which I had never gotten a man's perspective before.

As time passed, we traveled to and fro by car and plane, continuing to discuss future possibilities of our work. The early days with him were an interesting learning experience for me. In fact, just standing beside him was interesting in and of itself. He was 6' 3" and that was a pretty dog gone huge deal for me, since I was just 5' 10.7599693412" tall. But beyond his height and size, it was an amazing thing for me to even stand next to him knowing that I was in the presence of my mind regulator, in human form.

Until the perfect storm occurred, I had no way of knowing how such regulation would transform my life. However, on the day that it occurred, I had a problem. Oh yes, we had a huge problem. My 6' 3" 350-pound mind regulator summoned me to his office to talk about a bad decision that I had made, and I had to face the music. When he asked me the question, "Rodney, did this happen?" All I could do was stand up straight as the heat of accountability came all over my body. My throat tightened as I looked into his eyes knowing that when he asked that question, he already knew the answer. From that point it was just a matter of, "was I going to lie or was I going to tell the truth." The answer was easy. I was not going to lie. My countenance remained poised and respectful, while in my mind, I was asking, "Who in the world is this? Who is this person that has the nerve and the unmitigated gall to look at me and actually tell me what to do? Who are you? Who is he? Why is he? Where did he come from?" Well, after all of the ranting and raving, I knew the answer. The mind regulator came directly from the almighty God.

The truth was, I had let a wheel run off and for the first time in 30 years, my mind would be regulated and my life would change forever. All of a sudden, I was forced to stand up like a man, look at my life and say, "What am I doing?" because that kind of reality check is the type of thing that a man needs. A man needs a mind regulator. I needed a mind regulator and that is exactly what I got. Up until that point, I had only experienced and interacted with my grandmother's love in the time of crises, which usually occurred as a result of my reckless living. She had loved me, held me, fed me, and kissed me on the forehead, whenever I did something crazy, but she had never regulated my mind, because she could not do it. No matter what I did she made it all right.

The reason God made mothers and fathers is to satisfy the need for the child to see both sides of affection. As my grandmother was able to give me the love that was needed, my real father, in his absence, was not there to offset that love with direction and absolute authority. When love comes in daily doses, it doesn't leave space for the emptiness of heart. However, when the emptiness of heart is present in daily doses, it leaves a hole that we sometimes attempt to cover.

The mind regulator was the only person that could have gotten my attention, because true regulation from a man comes without caring about tears and manufactured pain. Men are conditioned to be tough and are made to receive direction by more intensely paying attention to a deeper tone and voice. For it is the lower decibels of speech that reveal the layer of manhood that is needed for growth and true understanding.

Hearing my grandmother say, "Sit down," sounded completely different than when it came from the expanded vocal chords of my grandfather. When man meets boy, the authority in that exchange is clear and undeniable. The respect that a boy has for his father is often shown in a tear, and as correction pushes a tear out of a boy's eye, it falls on firm ground of unmovable love.

I knew that I loved my grandfather, when his voice of disappointment alone could bring me to my knees, without the touch of his heavy hand of discipline. He could look at me and say just a few words and I would crumble with emotion from the depth and controlled power of his voice. However, because he was not there all the time to consistently provide the doses of direction to offset my grandmother's love, I don't believe that I became the person that I could have become. On a daily basis, my fight of living up to an expectation that was never set continues. Without a father or a strong voice of any kind, I set my own parameters and goals in the loneliness of my days. Yes, I have always said that I really didn't miss having a father around, because I had my grandmother's love and faith to carry me. However, I will admit that the place in which my father was made to reside is held in limbo for the day that he steps into the scene. No matter how young or old a man may be, the need for his father is ever present.

As I have shared already, I got a whole lot from being in the presence of my grandmother, but once my grandfather died I was really left to my own devices. My actions showed it and my heart continues to mask it daily as I matriculate through life, pressing my way to a future filled with unknown possibilities. My grandmother's faith was enough to enable me to achieve my present place in life, but my father's faith would have been masterful in providing the necessary balance to create a perfectly well rounded, mature man.

As I write this chapter, my only son and his wife are expecting their first child. It is my hope that I can be a better addition to his child's, my grandchild's, regulation than I was to his mind regulation. Some would say that we make our own bed and that as adults we are responsible for creating lives that are full and worthy of respect whether a father was or was not present in our lives. I say that we all are different human beings with creative minds that are housed in the cavity of our skulls. We all need love and mind regulation in equal measure.

Farther Along

By
Rev. W.A. Fletcher

Farther along we'll know all about it
Farther along we'll understand why
Cheer up my brother live in the sunshine
We'll understand it all by and by

When we see Jesus coming in glory
When he comes down from his home in the sky
Then we shall meet him in that bright mansion
We'll understand it all by and by

Farther along we'll know all about it
Farther along we'll understand why
Cheer up my brother live in the sunshine
We'll understand it all by and by

Chapter Seven: The Great Debate

I think of myself as being a quintessential Renaissance man. When I attempt to explain to others how my individual talents were initially noticed or unlocked in my mind, and try to pinpoint the date when they awakened in my consciousness, there is always a connection to my childhood. As a child, I played with paper, pencils, and pens, when visiting my birth mother's office at the Social Security Administration. Usually, I was allowed to play on the table in the break room. All of her co-workers knew that when little Rodney was there that they made sure that there was plenty of paper, pencils, and pens available for my use. The office environment was a perfect playroom for my mind, because it had all of the supplies that I needed to be creative. That particular time proved to be very beneficial to me in life, because as a creative person, anything that I see, touch, and experience goes into my mental database. There, it is stored for later use, which could come on any given day, at any given time, and under any given circumstance.

    Some time ago, I made the Renaissance man statement to a friend, who found it to be an arrogant declaration. She joked that, in her opinion, I more closely resembled Tarzan, the king of the jungle, wearing a tool belt and playing a grand piano, rather than Michelangelo, the artist, sculptor, painter, architect, poet, and engineer, who painted the magnificent Sistine Chapel in the Vatican City and sculpted David, who presently resides in the Galleria dell'Accademia di Firenze in Florence, Italy. Of course I disagreed with her comparison, but agreed that she was entitled to her opinion. I view my similarities quite differently based upon my understanding of a Renaissance man and the particular set of skills that I possess.

My idea of a Renaissance man is pretty straightforward. He embodies a strong desire to learn as much as possible about as many things as possible. He does not limit himself to the realm of dexterity, but allows his mind to soar to the outer realms of the universe. Whether that entails astronomy or abstract thought that includes creative design and innovation, he cannot be pigeonholed, because his mind is bigger than the box that would contain his perceived ability. Given a block of wood, a Renaissance man will see the possibility inside before picking up a tool to complete the woodworking process. Using a canvas, the masterpiece is already designed, virtually in his mind, before the pen or brush makes the first stroke. Given a chord, a melody automatically leaps into his mind along with the lyrical prose of a beautiful song. When working towards an endpoint, night turns into day and day turns into night, because he is not bound by the clock and time. If he sets his mind to a task, you had better believe that he is going to work every point in the project schedule to get to the finale.

As a Renaissance man, I spend a lot of time alone, and sometimes, work best alone, because in the creative process, the specificity of what I am doing can be easily interrupted by the mere presence of other people in the workspace. I find that, oftentimes, when creating art pieces, quietness and stillness is needed to allow the creative thought process to be birthed and carried through to the revelation of a unique gift to the world. When I am creating something that I have never seen or even worked on before, I need to be alone to let the organic process develop in that space between my conscious and unconscious mind. On these occasions, often by happy accident, everything that I have ever seen in my lifetime comes into play when a whole new body of information, which had been previously hidden in my mind, is revealed with one conversation. To borrow from one of my favorite Bible verses, eye hath not seen and ear has not heard what is possible for the Renaissance man, who is moved by the Holy Spirit, towards his appointed destination.

In 1998, I became the Minister of Music of a large Methodist Church in Dallas, Texas. The church had a 9-foot Steinway piano that was positioned on the floor, too far away from the choir. I felt that it needed to be moved and elevated. I discussed this observation with the pastor and church leadership, and they agreed to make it happen. Thanks to skills stored in my mental Rolodex during childhood play, I was able to tape off the floor exactly where the piano should be placed, and develop the specifications for a riser, or small stage, to place it on. For the sake of symmetry, I also designed a plant display case on the opposite side, because symmetry plays a large role in the way I think about design and art. I just don't like for things to be unbalanced. When my design was completed, fellow choir member, Floyd Jones headed a four-person carpentry crew to build it, and the project turned out very well.

Following the completion of the piano stage, the associate pastor asked me to create a bookshelf in a stairway in his new home. Although I agreed to construct it, I did not have a clue of how it was to be done. I did know that if I could imagine it, then I could create it, or at least come up with a buildable concept. I needed help and I knew just who to ask. His name was Floyd Jones. Floyd, who had headed up the piano stage build out, was a retired trim carpenter, who had begun working as a general manager for a large construction company. I asked him to show me a few little things about carpentry, which would allow me to construct the small project. He agreed to do so and invited me over to his home.

When I entered Floyd's garage, I was simply amazed. The garage contained all of the tools and nomenclatures that were used in his previous occupation as a trim carpenter. Trim carpenters are also known as finish carpenters, because they typically complete the project with the final carpentry details, thereby making the job looked finished. Trim carpentry, the work that a trim carpenter performs, requires precision measuring and cutting to create a seamless finished appearance. A trim carpenter's mind must be specific in nature, because there is a real and significant difference between 1 inch, 1/2 inch, 1/4 inch, 3/8 inch, 1/16 inch, and 1/8 inch. What better realm of existence for the creative mind, than to be driven toward ultimate perfection, exhibited in an aesthetically pleasing finished product.

The conversation/carpentry lesson lasted less than an hour. During the short period of time, Floyd taught me enough about carpentry to launch my mind into a whirlwind of ideas that would lead to a successful career in the field. I learned many things including how to use a chop saw, also know as a miter saw, and a miter box. My assignment for that day was to create a box, with a face frame that could slide in a drywall cut out between two studs in a wall, and hold books that were to be placed on its shelves.

During my hour with Floyd, I discovered that a whole new world existed in my brain. It was as if a pen had popped a sack of knowledge that had been implanted in my mind from those days in my mother's break room. I would make squares, cubes, triangles, octagons, hexagons, things for my trucks, things to hold pins at my desk at school, and pockets to store information made out of paper, which hung off the end of my little wood and metal desk at school. I created all types of things during that time. As a result of my experience, I reached the conclusion that the repetition of one's activities as a child is stored in the mind for later use.

When I had that conversation with Floyd about wood and how to cut 45° angles, I was able to channel my eight-year-old self and pull all of that information that had been stored, while cutting paper and using scissors and tape. Although, as an adult, I was no longer using scissors and tape, I was applying the exact same principles to wood, nails, glue, clamps and all types of different materials.

The visit with Floyd on that day began what I like to call the great debate. It began with a conversation about carpentry, and since I was merely a musician and a singer, Floyd had no idea that he was dealing with a Renaissance man. He did not know that he was dealing with a man with abilities that had been lying dormant since childhood, waiting for just the right conversation to awaken them. Floyd did not know, and neither did I, that the great debate, between music and carpentry, had started that day, or that carpentry would be the occupation in which I would excel for the next 15 to 20 years of my life.

In the days, weeks, and months following our visit, I found myself having to figure out whether the very thing that I thought that I was, which was a singer and a musician, was starting to become a distraction. My new interest was carpentry. Carpentry is one of those things that require one's undivided attention, because there is a little rule in carpentry, called measure twice cut once. It is necessary to follow this rule, because sometimes one only has enough wood to complete the project at hand. At other times, the wood is so exotic, and so special, that it is only available in limited quantities. Due to its price point, accuracy in cutting is imperative, so again, it must be measured twice and only one cut is possible. There are no second chances or "do over's" allowed in this game.

Before I realized what was happening, carpentry needed all of my time, and so did my current job as the Minister of Music of the large church. The two cerebral hemispheres of my brain were literally divided. With one side, I found myself coming to choir rehearsal in cargo shorts and boots, directing anthems and creating morning hymns, along with directing songs and preparing musicians for the Sunday services. On the other side, I was thinking about creating a handmade gazebo for one of the church members, or creating the drum cage for the sanctuary to damper the sound of the snare drum bouncing off of the brick walls of the new edifice in which we were standing during the choir practices.

It is amazing how one can be looking straight ahead while the mind is looking in two different directions. To me, that kind of thinking brushed up very closely to complete insanity. That realization alone to me was a very dangerous and a very scary place to be at the moment. To think that music, the very thing that I had loved all of my life, the very thing that Mamma had invested her money and time in for me, for eleven years, was a distraction! Was I really crazy? So ensued the great debate between music and carpentry.

The winner of the debate, at least temporarily, was carpentry. Carpentry took over my mind and I began to create amazing things. I built a bedroom set from scratch for myself and began to make things for other people. I created gazebos, cabinets, chairs, and all types of things for people to use in their homes. I found carpentry to be extremely exhilarating, because it allowed me to use all of the skills that I had stored in my mind. It was amazing for me to be able to experience all of these challenges and to solve my own questions. It was a challenge, because it went from a one-hour lesson and deciding that I was not going to sing or play, to becoming a carpenter. Carpentry inundated my thoughts and mind and took over my whole being as I traveled, all over the United States, building things for people. By the age of 35, I was creating projects that were totally outside of anything that I would have ever imagined. I was really excited and really up for almost any challenge. By the age of 45, I was on Home & Garden Television (HGTV), competing as one of the top handymen in America.

Although I took on any and every kind of carpentry opportunity with gusto and fervor, the great debate between music and carpentry was ever present. No matter where I was, or what I was creating, there standing in the corner of my mind, was music. Music was and has always been jealous, because it was the thing that hit my mind first. During the many years, since the great debate began, music has stood by silently whispering in my hear, "how in the world can you leave me by myself, to my own devices, when I am the reason that you are even aware of this church that you stand in, or of the person that you are working for, or of the projects that you are creating?"

As the years passed, Music's voice became louder and louder, a virtual crescendo in my mind. Eventually it became aggressive and began saying aloud, "Renaissance man, what about me?" "How could you leave me when I was your first love?" People would come up to me and say, "you don't sing anymore," but little did they know that even though I said, "no, I don't have time," Music was standing on my shoulder, and tapping me on the head with its director's baton of time saying, "how dare you say you don't have time for music, when I am the reason that you got into carpentry." That's the great thing about life; it shows us our deepest selves in vivid color, just when we need to see it. My life has been a microcosm of, if it had not been for —then this would not be. Music has haunted me every day.

The great debate occurs, because a Renaissance man has two competing switches that control the thought tracks in his mind. However, the mind can only purely operate on one switch at any given moment. Since skills are funneled into the brain, they are molded equally by the senses. Each one of the skills wants the same things. Each wants the same hands. Each wants to use the same eyes. Each wants to use the same body to create whatever it is that is applied to its nature. One sure thing is that a Renaissance man must be able to handle all of those skills at one time with the greatest of ease, and that in and of itself is a skill.

The great debate was an experience that helped me to understand that everything is important and each skill set deserves my attention. Being a Renaissance man has helped me to understand that if I follow God's Lead, I will arrive safely and sanely at my destination.

Lead Me, Guide Me

by
Doris M. Akers

I am weak and I need Thy strength and power
To help me over my darkest hour
For just open my eyes that I may see
Lead me oh Lord, won't you lead me

Lead me, guide me along the way
For if you lead me I cannot stray
Lord let me walk, Each day with thee
Lead me oh Lord, won't you lead me

I am lost if you take your hand from me
I am blind without thy light to see
Lord just always let me Thy servant be
Lead me oh Lord, won't you lead me

Lead me, guide me along the way
For if you lead me I cannot stray
Lord just open my eyes that I may see
Lead me oh Lord, won't you lead me.

Rodney Dean Boyden

My mom Doris Boyden McCormick

Rev. & Mrs. R.I. Brown

Piano Teacher Mrs. Bessie Smoot

My Grandmother's Faith

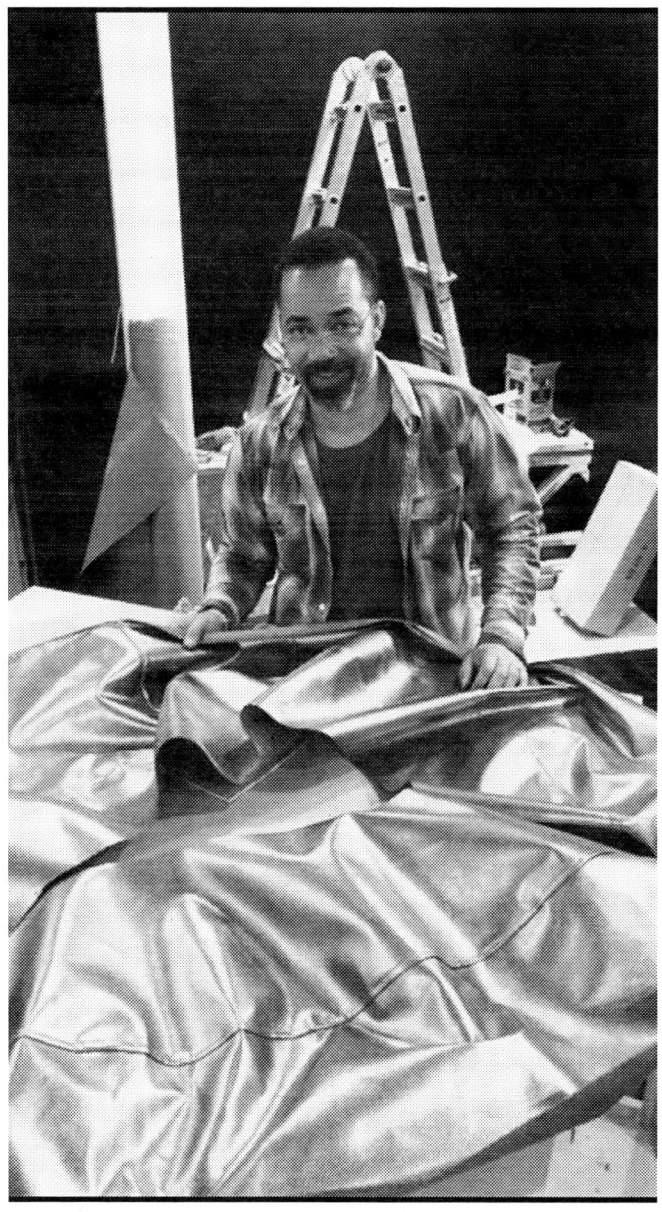

The Interior Designer

Rodney Dean Boyden

My son Christopher

My Grandmother's Faith

Mike Holmes and Scott McGillivray, HGTV

Rodney Dean Boyden

Mike Holmes on HGTV

Bishop and First Lady T. D. Jakes

Rodney at 50 & 14

My Grandmother's Faith

My son and daughter-in-law Christopher and Lisa Kirkpatrick

Rodney Dean Boyden

My son Christopher and his mother Dr. Cassandra Kirkpatrick

My Grandmother's Faith

My everyday high school attire

Rodney Dean Boyden

Woman Thou Art Loosed Gospel Play

Chapter Eight: Thriving Behind the Scenes

Point blank, this chapter has been titled "thriving behind the scenes." While this title will be discussed in great detail, in actuality I want to communicate the importance of self-confidence. I define self-confidence as that "something" that you feel inside when you know that you have the ability to match any task. I am not talking about having a super inflated ego or a big head about something, but I'm talking about that quiet, calm, peace of mind that comes when you know who you are and you can say, "I've got this situation under control."

Confidence has played a humongous role in my ability to make it through the various situations that I have encountered in my life. Without it, I would have crumbled into millions of pieces. I also credit confidence for enabling me to navigate through the perils of people's attitudes, mindsets, and false perceptions of me. Without it, I would have just turned into a shell of nothingness and felt as though I was equal to the paint that covers the dotted lines and dashes that people roll by each day in the middle of the highway.

As a little boy, my grandmother gave me a lot of confidence and she gave it to me in ways that made me feel special. She told and showed me that I was important, of great value like gold, and that I was special. I am not necessarily saying that her way was the only way or the best way to do it, but I do know that just telling children that they are special is not enough. Children have to feel the love that comes from parents or guardians, so that they know that they are special and that is exactly what happened in my life. I remember the times that we walked while holding hands, talking, laughing, and smiling at each other. When she talked to me, I saw in her eyes that she felt that she was talking to someone who was important enough for her to spend her time engaging in a conversation.

The confidence that she gave me propelled me to excel in piano and started me on the path of being on stage. I sang at the first funeral when I was eight years old and started playing for Sunday school at the age of nine. The performances never stopped and I've been on stage in front of people and the bright lights most of my life.

In previous chapters I mentioned that I possess many creative gifts and talents including acting, which led me to several theatrical opportunities, the first of which was a touring gospel stage play. One day I received a call from the play's writer asking me to audition for the role of lead male singer. It was not uncommon for me to receive these calls when a singer was needed to sing high notes, and I've always been puzzled by that, because I don't really sing high. However, they called me anyway.

This show initially ran in Los Angeles and was rewritten for a national tour, but the actor who originally had the leading role that I was auditioning for, was no longer a part of the cast. Upon entering the room for the audition, I was greeted by a well-known playwright as well as the wife of the author who wrote the book from which the play was adapted. The playwright said, "Well, could you sing something?" and I said "sure." So, I sang a little something. When I finished he said, "That's good," and I said, 'Well thank you, I appreciate that." Now, the author's wife had heard me sing many times before and she already knew that I could sing well, which was the reason that they called me in the first place. The playwright looked at me and said, "Do you think that you would be able to go on the road with our show?" Now the average person would think that a jubilant "yes" and resounding, "Oh my god I can't wait," would have been my answer, but it was not. I simply paused to think about the offer.

You see, at the time of the audition, I was employed as the Minister of Music for a church in a large metropolitan city with a consistent paycheck coming in every week. I had an office, parking space with my position on it and a 401k. I also owned a house with a pool and a dog. Life was good for me and I had finally landed in a place where I could actually grow and dream.

I was appreciative for this new theatrical opportunity, because it had come years after the incident with the Mind Regulator, which resulted in some life-changing consequences. Life had dealt me traumatic blows, but after all that I had been through, I was satisfied. So, when I answered, "It depends," the playwright looked at me like I was crazy. I believed he misunderstood my response and interpreted my pause as arrogance. It wasn't that I was being arrogant. It wasn't that I was saying that, "I'd think about it", because I am Rodney Dean Boyden, but I was thinking about it, because I remember what I had just gone through to get to that present state in life. He had no idea of who I was or what I had dealt with before I met him on that day. He was just looking at what he thought he saw in the person standing in front of him. He had no idea that what I looked like was not where I had been. Needless to say, my response did not go over too well.

After finalizing the particulars, I was selected to take the place of Ollie Woodson, the R&B recording artist who previously had the role. I became the new lead male character in the national touring play.

The play ran in theatres in every major city in America from California to New York and was at the Apollo Theatre for a month. The Apollo Theatre is the haut monde (high society), the crème de la crème of theatres in the African American community, and if you go and sing there, you have done it all.

Nobody in the touring group knew that I had sung at the Apollo five or six times before joining the play. Fresh out of high school in the 1980s, I used to drive to New York weekly to sing there on amateur nights just to be a part of the competitions. Returning to the historic stage with the play was a great opportunity and I was ecstatic.

Everything was good. I was on the stage in front of the lights singing my song every night to standing ovations, and the crowd cheered loudly, because I had a song that required me to hold a note for about 20 to 30 seconds every night. It was wonderful! When I was not singing, I was the bad guy in the show. This was really fun, because I had to be really mean and the audience booed me at curtain call each night. A lot of loud booing meant that I had done well.

At some point the promotion team decided to bring back Ollie Woodson, who was the guy that I had replaced. Since he had been a part of the "Temptations" singing group back in the day, they felt that having his name on the marquee would boost ticket sales when the show went to the Apollo. I admit that I was a little hot under the collar about the fact that they were going to replace me with the guy that they had fired, or who had quit, before I was hired. However, they insisted that they were going to have him come back in my place. So they replaced me with him for one night and much to their dismay, and surely much to his dismay, it didn't work. While he was gone, the character type changed, and his style did not work with the new flow of the production. Following the character change mishap, the director decided to keep me as lead, and I was grateful to have the job for the rest of the play's scheduled run.

A few years later the same playwright called and asked if I would do wardrobe for his current show. Now I need you to understand that this is where the rubber started meeting the road. I had never "done wardrobe" before and did not know what the position entailed. I thought that the playwright called, because he knew that I could sew and had other artistic abilities that could be used to make sure that everybody's clothes were straight.

So, in my mind I'm like yeah, I'll come, no problem. I vividly remember traveling to meet them in Memphis dressed in slacks, a blazer, nice shoes, funky socks, and a turtleneck. This was my normal choice of clothing, especially the turtlenecks, because they kept my neck warm in cold weather. This is basically how I dressed.

So, I was doing my job in my normal attire when someone walked by and said, "Who do you think you are?" I responded, "What do you mean, who do I think I am? "Nobody, I'm just working." He said, "Why are you dressed like that?" I said, "This is just how I dress." He said, "Well you don't need to dress like that. That isn't how you're supposed to dress." Now of course, I am Rodney and I was just about to start feeling a certain kind of way, because that was the first time that I felt that someone was actually trying to diminish me as a person. I'm like, "who cares how I dress as long as I'm doing what I'm supposed to do?" I'm thinking that my clothes are fine, as long as I'm doing my job, and as far as I knew I was doing a fine job. However, that interaction helped me to understand that when people are not comfortable with your self-perception they inform you or try to make you think that you are not who you think you are.

I don't necessarily know or remember if I immediately changed how I dressed. In fact, I don't know if I changed how I dressed for the entire run of that particular show. It might have switched to jeans and boots in the weather, but I was getting my job done. Just understand that this exchange created an atmosphere that was not conducive to my being a popular part of the cast or the crew, because the perception was that I was arrogant and conceited.

Their thoughts of me even showed one evening when I filled in for one of the background singers. During one of the meetings between shows, they proclaimed that I had allowed an incorrect note to exit my mouth. This immediately enraged the composer, music director, songwriter, music teacher, choral director, and pianist inside of me. For the ability for me to sing a wrong note lies outside of the realm of probability. I proclaimed loudly and emphatically, in the meeting, that their observation was incorrect. I may have displayed a teaspoon of arrogance for that moment for the protection and integrity of my musical abilities. The fact is, there are only three notes in the triad of a chord, and if I did happen to sing a note that was different than the previous background singer, it fell within the structure and key of the song that was being performed. In other words, they had gone too far!

On other occasions, while attempting to fit in with the cast, I was even accused of two crimes. One involved food poisoning, and the other was a set-up. The food poisoning incident occurred in New Orleans with one of the show's leading characters. After shopping for her wardrobe, I suggested that we eat at the local food court, where we had Chinese Noodles. The meal caused her great digestive discomfort, which was used by the star of the show for an additional amount of comic relief. I must say that would prove to be one of the best shows, because of that situation.

The second incident was a set-up whereby I was given tickets to the Oprah Winfrey Show in Chicago and chose two friends to accompany me. The guests that day included Bernie Mac and Chris Rock. One of my friends shared the fact that we were there from a traveling gospel play and there began a downward spiral. Upon becoming aware of our attendance, Bernie Mac said, "you know you want to sing, because all of you gospel people are always somewhere trying to sing." In a skittish, apprehensive voice my friend said, "No, I don't want to really sing," as she began to belt out a verse of her favorite gospel song. Needless to say, Chris Rock pounced on her rendering without hesitation. This comedic exchange was again shared with our show's leadership and I was blamed. Even though these instances were comedic in nature, to me they spoke to a larger narrative. Some people will use the negative in situations to support their argument of devaluing you as a person. This tactic is only effective when you can't see that they are masking their lack of an equal level of self worth.

Because I was wardrobe, they wanted to somehow keep me in some sort of subservient and uninformed position. However, I wasn't having any of that "on the job oppression." Most of the people in this production were not aware of any of my abilities, so they were treating me as just another person behind the scenes with skills only in that particular area. Truth be told, they were attempting to call me out on the subject of music, of which I was completely aware. I would have received their discontent better, if it had been related to my lack of knowledge in the wardrobe position, because that is where my true deficiency was present.

Imagine me running around doing stuff that I've never done in my life and didn't know that I was going to be doing at any point in this lifetime. Imagine a grown man going into Eckerd's Drug Store asking, "Where are the eyelashes?" Imagine a grown man going into the J.C. Penny's Department Store looking for Bobby Brown Derma Blend. Imagine a grown man walking into a beauty supply store asking for wigs, the long hooker and the gray old lady types. Imagine a grown man walking in any store looking for the women's scented lotion and stockings in the little eggs, because the women in the touring group like to wear those little stockings in the show. For the highlight of this outlandish shopping spree, imagine a grown man walking into a women's shoe store asking, " do you have a size 14 flat shoe?" and adding, "and oh! I need them in black and blue." If I would have gotten pulled over and searched by the police, the items that I had just purchased would have been enough evidence to arrest me for a myriad of crimes including suspicion of prostitution and impersonation of a very large woman. In all actuality, I was actually putting my manhood on the line for this job. This work was ridiculous! Where in the hell had I ended up? How in the world did I arrive here?

To understand my journey, I had to go back and recall one of my first experiences watching production crews in action. In the theatre world there is a separation between on and off stage activity, which must be realized before one can be successful. The production staff has specific roles, which enable them to work in tandem, because they understand their assigned positions.

Thinking back on the separation between on and off stage activity, I recall a time when I was a minister of music. David, the actor who played Barney, the big purple dinosaur, was in the choir and invited us to visit him on the set to see what he did. So, few other church members and I went to watch him on the set. We were sitting there when all of sudden here comes Barney, dum didum dum dum. David in the big purple Barney suit was actually Barney. I noticed that when Barney came out, there was a leaf on the ground, which nobody on stage with Barney picked up. The production lady who was responsible for greenery went and got the leaf and placed it back on the set where it needed to be positioned. This was done for continuity, because the leaf that was visible one minute could not disappear during the next minute. Although I did not understand the significance of this observation until many years later, it proved to be my first lesson on crew etiquette.

Playing and looking your part is important to crew membership. With that experience etched in my memory, I can recall walking around in semi-casual wear while doing wardrobe and it hit me, I was not looking the part and I wasn't hanging with the correct group of people.

Because I set up an organized system of breaking down the dressing rooms, I was able to get all of the cast member's things together, packed up in the boxes, and at the stage door for loading by the time the cast was ready to leave. This allowed me to leave with the cast and not wait on the crew who would be there until the wee hours of the morning. Leaving with the cast fueled their perception of my arrogance. Failing to provide me a job description was a grand assumption on their part that I knew everything about my position and how it worked. In all actuality, I did not know very much about the job duties of the position.

I realized that I was part of a crew and that I had never been a crewmember before that time. I took in the backstage view of how the crew worked and began to understand that the crew does things differently. The cast is on the stage and the crew is off the stage living behind the scenes.

Crewmembers wear black clothes, shoes, pants and hats. They are very particular about their jobs and slide around behind the curtains in the dark. The crew is there to make sure everything works and is in its place. I laugh today just thinking about how it must have looked to them. As they worked, I was walking around looking like the director or the show's producer. How do you think that went over? Not good.

The show went on a few more months and I did my thing, knowing that the atmosphere and the energy around me was not conducive for me to continue. They didn't call me back on the next leg. Was I surprised? No.

I remember this experience and took it with me as a lesson learned when one of my friends asked me to go on the road with her new production as lead carpenter. The word "lead" and "carpenter" sounded exciting, because I would have the opportunity to lead people in carpentry. It sounded like the perfect thing for me. I had gotten a chance to see the people working behind the scenes making sure that the set was ready to go, painted and tightened up, so this time, I had experience as related to the job duties.

I just kept on living and the experience I gained along the way somehow worked to my benefit. I did not go into the next job blind, not knowing what I was expected to do. I went in with a new perspective, having already been there and done that type of work. I knew what behind the scenes was supposed to look like and oh what fun it was to do this job.

I hung out, ate, and traveled on the crew bus. I woke up and left for the venue with the crew at four and five in the morning to start the day. I went out for beers with the crew, because that's what a crewmember does after the job is completed. An interesting thing that I learned from this whole experience was that the after hours comradery of a group of people in any organized situation is paramount to the success of the working environment.

Our work had to be completed by the time the cast sashayed in with their high and mighty selves. Most of the time, they didn't even speak to us crewmembers, because they thought they were too good. Little did they know that I was once a cast member and was paying close attention to how they were treating me while behind the scenes. It showed me how I, in some cases, might have treated crewmembers when I was in the shoes of a cast member. To say the least, this was a teachable moment in my theatre life.

It was also an amazing thing to watch the cast walk by me as they stepped off of their tour bus at 5 p.m. each day, knowing that we had been working since 4 a.m. They walked onto the set as if they were saying, "We have arrived!" I loved watching this scene play out, because now they had made the mistake of allowing me to see both sides of this situation.

Now I had been schooled by a previous show on the etiquette of the crew attire. This time around, I, as the lead carpenter, was now happy to shop for the coolest black uniform that I could find. I also had every tool that I needed for the job organized and ready to go. At that juncture, I was thrilled being a crewmember.

The lesson I learned about understanding my place in life, and staying in my lane, was important. I came to realize that my self-worth was key as I accepted the truth that life has lanes with rules that apply to each person. The theatre experiences also taught me that the minute I got out of my lane for any reason, I could bump into the people beside me and step on toes. Self-confidence took the place of my need to prove myself to others and faith in God and myself kept me grounded. Therefore, when people attempted to put their foot on my head, it didn't offend or bother me. Humility needs no height, because it grows from having a solid foundation.

I also realized that behind the scenes, I could still be a shining light in the dark, because I am happy there in my awareness of self and circumstances. I gained an even greater sense of awareness when just being behind the scenes was replaced with thriving behind the scenes. It showed I had become one with the knowledge of the effect that I had on the bigger picture.

I understand that without the work behind the scenes, there would be no set to stand on, no furniture to sit on, no microphones to sing into, and no clothes to wear. We are all pieces of the puzzle that are required in order to make a complete picture. Just knowing I had all of the skills needed to step into any position and any role of the production was all I needed at that time. Accepting this fact about my work life gave me solace. It helped me to understand that I had enough self-confidence that the darkness of backstage was just as comfortable as the light of being on stage.

As I came to this place of the true message of understanding my first wardrobe job, I called the writer and the producer of that show to apologize for the way that I had handled myself in their workplace. I was glad to share my thoughts on the matter, because I believe that it clarified a lot of unanswered questions in both of our minds about that working relationship. Because of those honest conversations, we are friends to this day.

Now, as I prepare to set my own goals towards producing my own productions, I can relate to every aspect of the show. This includes being in the pit with the musicians, on the stage as an actor, and behind the stage as a crew member. I can write a job description for each of the positions.

This message is simple. I can thrive behind the scenes. I can stand up behind the scenes. I can thrive in my lane knowing that wherever I am, I can be who I am — tough, strong, and confident as I do my job very well. Now I can walk tall knowing as I ponder the thought, "Will they remember me when I'm gone?" the answer will be a resounding, "Yes!"

Confidence is when your gifts do more talking about you than you can do when talking about yourself.

Rodney Dean Boyden

This Little Light of Mine

By
Avis Burgeson Christiansen and
Harry Dixon Loes

This little light of mine
I'm going to let it shine
Oh, this little light of mine
I'm going to let it shine
Hallelujah
This little light of mine
I'm going to let it shine
Let it shine, let it shine, let it shine

Ev'ry where I go
I'm going to let it shine
Oh, ev'ry where I go
I'm going to let it shine
Hallelujah
Ev'ry where I go
I'm going to let it shine
Let it shine, let it shine, let it shine
All in my house

I'm going to let it shine
Oh, all in my house
I'm going to let it shine
Hallelujah
All in my house
I'm going to let it shine
Let it shine, let it shine, let it shine

Chapter Nine:
Attitude Under Pressure

When I was growing up, there were all types of situations where attitude raised its aggravating head. Adults always said, "Rodney, you have to have a good attitude." Teachers in school said, "Your attitude determines your altitude." Sometimes we kids would look at each other as if to say, "Who cares about attitude?" All we knew was that whatever it was that we wanted to do, "We Wanted To Do It!" We just wanted people to stay out of our way, and we insisted on making sure that we were able to have fun. We did not understand how attitude could have any bearing on our lives.

Well, the years have passed and life has taught me some valuable lessons. Now I know that attitude plays a major role in every aspect of life and it is the first thing that people notice about you. A bad attitude is like a flat tire. If you don't change it, you won't get anywhere. On the other hand, a good attitude allows you to get ahead of the fray in many ways. Not only must you strive to have a better disposition than the people around you, but you should possess a good attitude just for your own sanity.

I have often heard that it requires more muscles to frown than to smile. This means that when you are frowning, you're actually exerting more energy to create the look that you are trying to convey. You may think that you are scaring people and giving the impression that you are mean and not to be messed with. In all actuality, I believe that you are really showing them something you are not aware of at that moment. In many cases, you are demonstrating your own fear and insecurity about the situation or setting.

Another thing to consider is that your attitude does something to you inside, because a bad attitude causes you to look at life in a much more negative way than when you have a positive mindset. I always say that I love optimistic people, because optimists are "glass half full" people and pessimists are "glass half empty" people and they make me itch.

The optimistic thinker will say that you can do whatever you want to do, while the pessimistic person will say you can't do much of anything. Positive, optimistic, creative people can't remain around negative people for very long, because the negativity erodes the ability to have open-ended thoughts and an open mind. Creativity thrives on optimism.

Of all of the opportunities that I've had in my life, one instance stands out in my mind that I will never forget. I really enjoy telling this story, and I hope you find its details interesting. It is a highlight of my entire creative career, and once again illustrates my grandmother's faith in action through me. I desperately appreciated it because I was stepping into uncharted territory. You see, I was about to be sequestered in a hotel in Los Angeles, California with a group of people, from all different backgrounds throughout the United States, whom I had never met in my life.

One morning while working on a project in Atlanta, Georgia, I was drinking coffee in a shop. As I walked around the corner, splattered across the TV hanging on the wall were the words Handyman Competition. Of course, I have always loved competition and talent shows, because they pressure me to prove myself by being focused on a goal or prize. Talent shows required me to perform before strangers, who often judged me from head to toe.

The words "Handyman Competition" stood out to me and produced a major sensory overload. These words spoke to both sides of me: the handyman/carpenter side and the competitive side, because I love the pressure of competing.

After calling the number and figuring out where the auditions were to be held, I went down to the W Hotel in Atlanta, Georgia. There, I sat in a room with a bunch of strangers, amazed that the waiting process was not longer than it was, considering the number of people who were there for the auditions.

I looked around the room and wondered who the people were and what they knew. I wondered if they were better than me. When you think about things like this, you must make sure that you do not make the mistake of judging people by the way they look, because sometimes the "worst-looking" people are the smartest people.

There I was in this room with all of these men, women, husbands, wives and a few children. Mostly, they were people who looked like they had been in the world of carpentry all of their lives. When you know carpenters, you can tell the ones who have been doing it for a while, because you see fingernails that have been smashed by hammers, and hands weathered and worn by being in the sun hammering and nailing. Carpenters love plaid shirts, old jeans, and boots that are ragged from years of working. They love long hair, bandanas, and baseball caps turned backwards. Most of the people there had this sort of carpenter's shaggy look.

As I sat there, realizing that I was a musician guy whose hands don't even look like they had ever done any work, I could have easily felt out of place. Even right now, when I relive the moment in my mind, I know that my attitude had to be intact for me to comfortably blend into the scene and not stand out like a sore thumb, no pun intended. It would have been easy to walk right out of that room thinking I wasn't the right look or the right type of person for the competition.

However, a good attitude looks at the glass as half full and I figured that I just looked a little different than most, which might turn out to be an attribute that most of the competitors wouldn't possess.

I was nervous, because no matter what I've done or what I'm doing, there's a certain amount of nervousness that comes with being under pressure. Eventually, a young lady came in and announced, "The next person is Rodney Boyden."

My heart started to race just a little bit, and, without any preparation or warm up, I was sitting on a stool in a room of the hotel. There, the interview was about to happen in front of a little digital video camera. With me in that room were two very cute young ladies with bubbly and energetic personalities who had a very important assignment. Their job was to get footage out of me that was positive enough to get me chosen out of all the thousands of people, from around America, that had auditioned in the fifteen selected locations, which including New York, California, and Washington D.C.

The ladies and I had a good conversation and we were all smiling and laughing. The selection committee guidelines had asked me to create a little gadget before I came to the audition, which showed how to do something in the world of carpentry. I constructed a little X-shaped box out of wood to demonstrate how to properly apply caulk to something. Caulking is very hard; you might think it to be very easy, but if you do it wrong, the outcome might look like a total mess and your project could be destroyed aesthetically as well as functionally.

With that little gadget, I was able to get their attention, because it was quite interesting, if I say so myself. On top of that, even though I was nervous and a little scared, I brought a great attitude into the room. This was something that I'm sure that they noticed, because they were having just as much fun as I was during this interview.

At the end of the interview, they said "We will contact you within two weeks, so just wait on a call."

So, I went on with my days and continued to do what I was doing there in the city. One day, my phone rang and it was HGTV calling me back. Now let me tell you, this was exciting! I made the cut and moved to the next round of interviews, which took place in New York. So, I got a plane ticket, packed my little bag, and jumped on a plane from Atlanta to New York City so that I could participate in this interview.

Anybody who knows New York City knows that it is a very large place. It's the type of city that, on your arrival, can be totally overwhelming from the magnitude of the buildings and number of people hustling and bustling along the streets. The hundreds of thousands of private cars, cabs, and stores that make up the big city can also make you feel very small very quickly. Frank Sinatra sang, "if you can make it there, you can make it anywhere," and I believe that to be the honest truth.

As I stepped into the interview room, I instantly noticed that it was full of cameras and there were about six to eight staff members waiting for me to come into the room. The situation was totally nerve-wracking, but I knew that I had to do a good job because these moments would determine whether or not I made the show as a cast member.

The group said, "Hi, Rodney." As I stood there, with all the confidence that I could muster and my grandmother's faith on the inside, I knew that I had to represent all that she had done for me. Also, I had to present myself in the most positive manner that I could. I said, "Hello."

Now I like to joke, and I wanted to cut the ice by saying something really crazy and off-the-cuff, so I exclaimed, "Why are you doing this to me and what do you want?" Well of course, they laughed because that was, I'm sure, the first such response that they had heard, but it worked. I wanted them to know that this was a way for us to all come back to earth by smiling and having a great laugh before the interview began.

I don't know how to explain this concept to you, if you're not familiar with the world of carpentry, but they were able to come up with a wooden puzzle, and each interviewee had only 15 minutes to complete the task. If you were not a good carpenter and if you had never encountered tools, angles, cutting, pencil drawing, and all of that necessary stuff, then you would have failed miserably on this particular test.

The most important thing to understand about this test was that the main ingredient, of these 15 minutes of interviewing, was pressure. I know that some of you think I repeat myself at times, but I must repeat the word pressure — pressure, pressure, pressure, because if you only say it once, it doesn't have the right effect.

So, I began to work this puzzle and not only was I able to complete it, but I was able to make it through the process with flying colors. Once completed they said, "Thank you very much, we look forward to speaking with you again if you make the cut." That left me in New York City with the rest of the day to ponder how I did, what they thought of me, and whether or not I would make it. I was nervous and worried, but one thing that I can say is that I left those people with this undeniable fact: the room had a better energy level than when I walked in, because everyone was smiling and I was able to smile along with them.

A few weeks later my phone rang once again and it was a staff member from HGTV informing me that I had been chosen as one of the ten best handymen in America. I was in total shock. Out of all of those people who signed up from all around America, my skill, confidence, and good attitude had taken me to the top of the heap with less than ten years of carpentry experience. I was overwhelmed with excitement and headed to Los Angeles for the competition.

In L.A., I met all of the contestants and the sizing up of the competition began in earnest. We were smiling, laughing and scanning each other like airport bomb detectors. Let me just say, I felt completely at home and confident.

The actual competition began a few days later and our lives and skills were put through the gauntlet of expectation and delivery. The HGTV team created all types of puzzles, scenarios, and situations with the goal of driving us completely bonkers. For the next three weeks, it was going to be all about pressure, which I believe to be the oxymoron of Pure, Exciting HELL!!

Just to give you an idea, the first task was to see who could completely install a new toilet in the fastest time, including whether the toilet would flush, and whether it would remain leak-free during the testing phase. Most of you, my dear friends, who have never put in a toilet really have no idea how easy it is to install if you are an experienced handyman. In this situation, however, we were thrust into the need to complete the job in 30 minutes without spilling any water or making any messes. Then, we had to uninstall the toilet, pack up, and clean up. It was like somebody plugged us into a 240 volt outlet and we could have absolutely lost our minds.

One thing that I can say with complete certainty is that when you really know what you know about a topic, that kind of pressure does not cause you to freak out and become overly anxious about the unknown. Usually people freak out because they are uncomfortable with what they don't know. However, the calm that comes over you when your skills are intact pushes your fear out of the way says to it, "Scoot back, because I've got this."

You don't realize it at the moment, but when you have been overtaken by your own skill, you are on, what I call, "autopilot." Autopilot is recalling what you know when you need to know it without thinking and that is what was happening to me at that time in the show.

Unfortunately for some, this day was the beginning of what I call the "weeding out" week. This particular task showed us immediately who was aware and who was not aware of certain scenarios and situations as they related to homebuilding and construction.

This show was going to press me into places that I had never been at any point in my short life. It was hilarious, but it was also completely shocking and nerve-wracking. Still, all that I can say is that on the first task, I stood firmly in my second-place spot just knowing that these people had messed up by letting me into this room. I was confident that my confidence and my great attitude were going to cause me to stand out as victorious as we continued through the rest of this competition. It was a great feeling to know, at that point, that I was up for the challenge and that the show was going to be fun.

We continued to work hard during the challenges, because being with strangers under pressure brought out all types of personality quirks. I had to make sure to keep a good attitude, because a bad one could have caused a tense situation to arise. As a group, we were able to keep good lines of communication open among ourselves, at least until we started getting down to the end.

As soon as we got down to 6-5-4-3-2 contestants, each contestant knew that things were getting tight and somebody had to go home. We continued to watch as contestants dropped like flies simply because of their mistakes. Those were some of the most demoralizing situations that we had during eliminations.

I competed until the fourth of the six episodes before getting eliminated alongside my team member. When we got to the last episode, this is where my attitude really showed its value while interacting with others in a competitive setting.

We were brought back in to the studio to watch the last two contestants on the finale, because on that day, somebody was going to win. I had bought some cool jeans while I was in California, so I was sitting there wearing a white T-shirt, jeans, and boots. I was ready to just sit back and watch TV as I observed this whole fantastic situation go down live, right before my eyes. Suddenly, the crew motioned that the show was ready to tape. Like the other former contestants, I had not come to work that day. However, because of my energy and skills, Sonne, one of the two finalists, brought me back into the competition.

    Wow, this was a surprising move, but I heard God say, "I've got something up my sleeve for you to do and the only way that you can do this work is to continue to have that same good attitude that you carried throughout this whole show." I felt that I was about to do something great. All of a sudden, the heat came over my body and I felt myself turning into an Incredible Hulk-like state. I felt a little bit better at this point for being chosen to assist Sonne.

    Sonne was far behind in her design build and I knew that I could help her to successfully cross to the finish line in first place. She didn't have many cabinets or anything else installed. We had a great deal of work to do in order to catch up to the other team. Since kitchen installation and interior design work were my areas of expertise, this stroke of fate was my chance to really have fun on national television. Suddenly, the clock started ticking and the show's director said, "On your mark, get set…GO!"

During this period, the cameras recorded the way I responded to leadership, because it was time to work as a team member. It was all about following direct instructions in order to get the work done. The producers observed how Sonne directed me, but they were also watching how I responded to direction.

Sonne said, "Okay Rodney, I know that you're good at this task, so I want you to create something that nobody else has produced. If you can do that for me, that would be great." I said, "You just said the right words, sister," and the next thing I can remember is taking off like Superman.

I was running around that set like a crazy person, because she had put me in the middle of my element. No longer was I kicked off the show. They had made a mistake and put me right back in the middle of the action and my confidence and skills rushed up in my brain.

While Sonne was over there doing her tasks, I was designing and building the island in the middle of the kitchen. Even though they tried to question me on my installation process, I knew that this tactic was just a ploy in order to see just how I would take criticism under pressure. I also knew that they were watching and evaluating me, so I still had to remain focused and keep it together.

Sonne and I worked like a well-oiled machine. As the clock ticked down to the end of the last four hours of the show, time was running out. We didn't pay any attention because we were too busy working as a team. Sonne was telling me what she needed in order to complete the contest, and I was following her lead without any resistance.

I was very glad to still be in the competition. I had enough confidence to know that I didn't need to be in a leadership role in order to be an effective team member. I could be a team member, have respect for Sonne's requests, and still do my job with a smile on my face. I was sweating like a wet rag on the beach and I felt like I was about to die, but I had to do my part to complete this show on a winning note. The clock came down to the last second and everybody was clapping, screaming, and hollering. So, picture this scene — I was moving, throwing, and putting stuff in place and as Sonne finished her last few tasks, and I began decorating the project space. We had basically completed our entire kitchen as the countdown of 5,4,3,2,1; STOP was heard in the room. As a team, we had accomplished the impossible by working together as an effective and productive unit.

So, we left the project room and I cleaned up before returning to the cast room. When I returned to the cast room, everybody was just in amazement and buzzing about witnessing one of the greatest comebacks in competitive show history.

This was our last time in the elimination room and on this day, the winner would be chosen. We stood there as teams and the finalists thanked us for our help in this last task.

I saw first-hand on this day that sometimes in life, even though you are ahead, you can make the wrong decisions, and it can come back to bite you in your proverbial "tail." Earlier, I had expected to be chosen by Scott, who was the other finalist and frontrunner. In my opinion, he had underestimated my ability and made the wrong choice by not choosing me for the final project.

As the judging team moved over to start evaluating Sonne, the judge said, "Sonne, the one thing that we liked was that you and Rodney worked well as a team. Your skill set might not have been as great, but you were trying your best to lead. It seemed as though you had a plan, and you chose the right person who could take your plan and put it into motion.

All of the contestants stood back there in complete shock, because we felt for just one small moment that something was about to happen that would be unprecedented. We knew that we were all learning a lesson that day that was much greater than HGTV and much greater than this hammer and nails competition. The practical lessons of the story were much greater than these cameras.

The judges deliberated as the trophy stood there in the middle of the room waiting to be presented to the winner. The contestants stood in dismay, shock, and total amazement at what the judges had just said. All of a sudden in the ticking time bomb of the moment, the judges declared Sonne as the winner.

My HGTV experience demonstrated that maintaining a good attitude under pressure is important and is the one thing that will carry you through life. It brought the underdog to becoming the top dog. When she held out the trophy, then we knew that she had won this entire competition, with a prize of $20,000. We each cheered!

On that day, I learned that if you stay calm and focused, redemption would follow you as though an invisible rope of inevitability were tied to you. She looked at me and she said, "Rodney, I thank you for helping me. I thank you for being there and doing all that you did to help, and for that I am giving you a portion of my winnings." That was an amazing gesture.

Attitude under pressure is what God loves, because it is a sign of faith in action and is what Jesus did when he carried the cross down the Via Dolorosa, "The Way of the Cross." I thank God for sending me down that path of lights, camera, and action to show me how to keep my mind on the prize of a higher calling. I thank God for sending me to this show to learn that a good attitude under pressure is a must — a requirement for a proper life. Once again, my grandmother's faith working in me proved to be the answer to the challenges that I had to face.

My Grandmother's Faith

Glory, Glory

By
The Byrds

Glory, Glory Hallelujah
Since I laid my burden down
Glory, Glory Hallelujah
Since I laid my burden down

I feel so much better
So much better
Since I laid my burden down
I feel so much better
So much better
Since I laid my burden down

Glory, Glory Hallelujah
Since I laid my burden down
Glory, Glory Hallelujah
Since I laid my burden down

Thank you Jesus, Thank you Jesus
Help me lay my burden down
I wanna thank you Jesus, thank you Jesus
Help me lay my burden down

Glory, Glory Hallelujah
Since I laid my burden down
Glory, Glory Hallelujah
Since I laid my burden down

Rodney Dean Boyden

Chapter Ten:
Mind, Material and Machine

From whence does knowledge and intellect derive? Does it come from the universal ether or is it imported from a higher ordered mind? We are told that all materials are composed of atoms traveling through space and time, and in specific instances the atoms combine to become the elements that we see in the physical realm. The Mind, Material, and Machine are obviously controlled by atomic interactions that are ordered in such a way as to benefit all humankind.

Thinking things through is an art, and finished projects have stages that are very important. When building or creating things, I must always be aware of where and how everything fits for correct assembly and I start at the end to get to the beginning, because the beginning is what you enjoy as a finished product. I refer to it as the negative sequential assemblage of any item or object.

Some visual artists will start an abstract piece having no idea where they are going. Because this is a single dimension thought process on canvas, it does not have to have an end result. Only the artist determines the finished product. In galleries, I have seen art creations sell for thousands of dollars that looked as though paint had been thrown at the canvas. To the artist, however, it was finished because there was no particular end result.

What is it like to have a brain that can comprehend the interactions behind so many materials and machines? This chapter shares several examples of exciting relationships in which using my mind, material, and machine enabled me to manifest unique designs on completely different platforms.

At around the age of sixteen, I was visiting a friend and a clock fell from the wall. Upon hitting the floor, the clock shattered into many pieces that some would have considered trash. I saw it as a challenge. Fortunately, because all of the broken pieces were present, I was able to gather them and repair the clock. At a moment's notice, I put my mind in action to reassemble the clock's pins and gears without any prior knowledge of the mechanism's original construction and it worked for many more years.

These types of opportunities presented themselves repeatedly, and addressing them became the norm for me. Over the years, I welcomed each occurrence that stretched my mind and gave me a reason to understand the inner workings of many things.

Early on, I learned that it is all about the tools. As such, I spent many years exploring tools and their connections to materials and machines. I explored the how and why of every tool that I could get my hands on. Whether creating, repairing or destroying something, I came to understand that the types of tools selected made all of the difference in a successful project.

Growing up, I was a good dresser and my grandmother made sure that I had all the stylish shoes and clothing that I needed. I especially enjoyed collecting Nike and other brand name tennis shoes because they came in cool colors. I can still remember my first wonderful pair, which I placed in the chair at the corner of my bed just so I could stare at them while falling asleep.

The difference between the average kid and me was inspiration. I not only saw the Nikes, but I also saw myself in a sweat suit that was color-coordinated with them. The local basketball teams were known for having matching sweat suits for uniformity, but I took it to a completely different level. Since stores in my town did not always sell sweat suits to match the shoes, I decided to design and sew my own. Fortunately for me, I had just the equipment needed to do it.

Coincidentally, some time earlier while playing on the porch, I discovered an old wooden deep cherry case with legs. Upon opening the lid, I found a black cast iron pedal-operated Singer Sewing Machine that was passed down to Mamma from her parents. I was instantly intrigued. After getting a few instructions from my grandmother on how to use it, I taught myself to sew.

My new sweat suit obsession meant that instead of going outside to play sandlot football or basketball in the evenings as I loved to do, I'd be in the house coming up with my next day's apparel. It was such an exciting time for me. I went to the fabric store and purchased gabardine material, which was a good and inexpensive fabric. Once I had the desired colors, I created a pattern, inserting blocking wherever I wanted a particular color on the garment.

I designed each garment by drawing it on paper and then making the pattern. After sewing all of the pieces together, the finished garment was set aside for my next school day. In the months to come, sewing became a normal part of my days, and most of the clothes in my closet were things I had designed and made.

This worked out just fine until the people realized that Rodney had not only been outside fixing his cars and bikes, but he was also making his own clothes. Suddenly, everything changed. When I first began sewing, I gave little thought to what the inside of a finished garment looked like, because I knew that I was the only one who was going to see it. My process was simple. I'd try the garment on, make sure that my seams and pockets lay flat and the buttonholes were in place. Next, I made sure that my sleeves and pant cuffs were even on both sides and I was "ready to go," or so I thought.

Once the people found out that I was making these clothes myself, something amazing happened. They started touching and grabbing my clothes and wanted to look on the inside of the garment. This was the funniest thing to me. When they did not know that I made the garments, just viewing the exterior was good enough. But, when they found out that I made it, the exterior alone was no longer acceptable, for it was the inside of the garment that validated my abilities.

At first, each time anyone reached to grab the garment to look on the inside, I jumped away. My speedy turn around time on sweat suit production was attributed to not putting linings in the clothes, because I did not want to take the extra time to sew them. I just wanted to get the outfit ready for the next day. The inside was not even on my radar.

Yes, I was afraid and did not want them to look inside my sweat suit, but after a short while, I decided to reevaluate my whole sewing *modus operandi*. When I began sewing, I was doing it fast and not taking the time to finish the whole garment from beginning to end. I was not closing up everything and making sure there were no loose strings.

My creations were wonderful on the outside, but chaos was usually breaking loose on the inside. It wasn't until people started grabbing my clothes that I felt the need to start making linings.

Anyone who knows anything about making linings can attest that the process is the same as making a second jacket. It has two sleeves, a back, front left and right panels, as does the outer layer. When I took the time to go through these extra steps, I found that it was liberating.

As the challenge of the sweat suit dissolved after years of mastering the particulars, my thoughts transferred to a much more challenging item. I began to design my own tailored men's suits. People commented all the time on how sharp I looked in my suits, and they had no idea that I was sewing them myself. Indeed, they would have been quite shocked to hear that after practicing the songs I needed for whichever church I was playing for, I was sewing suits and ties for myself and making matching dresses and clothing for the young lady I was dating at the same time.

Ladies, you haven't had a man until you can shop with him knowing that he can and will duplicate it all just for you overnight.

Once I started constructing the clothes properly, both inside and out, I could then walk around and just let the garment hang freely, open or closed. If they wanted to see what it looked like, I would say, "Yes, I made it, you want to see?" Sometimes, I did not even wait for them to grab it as they asked the question. I would unzip the jacket, take it off, and say, "Try it on." There was nothing better than knowing that I had taken the time to make sure that the inside of the garment was just as beautiful as the outside.

Using the jacket as a metaphor of life, how many of us are afraid for someone to get close enough to look and see who we really are on the inside? A lot of us are afraid for someone to grab our jackets and unzip our lives to see what is going on, because for some of us, chaos is breaking loose. I will tell you that there is a certain amount of pride that you get when you know you can flip the door to your life open and no matter what, whatever they see there is what it is.

I told the story of Floyd Jones and my first carpentry lesson, in the chapter on "The Great Debate." From that first lesson, as my carpentry skill set improved, I would build more things, including beautiful cabinets.

I noticed that every time I got better at building, something else came up that required me to add to the skill set that I already had. I learned that when dealing with wood, there are certain types of wood that can be cut certain ways with certain tools.

The materials that were needed for my previously mentioned creations varied. First, I sewed with gabardine, silks and other fabrics, and later I built with wood, glue and nails. In the same way that the material must fit together to construct a garment, the wood must go together to construct a cabinet. Just like with a garment, the way in which the cabinet goes together is crucial to how it looks in the end. The objective is to see nothing but seamless lines of wood attached together.

The final construction of a cabinet and a sweat suit adhere to the same scrutiny. Whether working as a tailor or a carpenter, when I make something, I want it to look pretty on both the inside and outside. I rub it and make sure it feels good, as well as functions in the proper manner.

The initial response to the knowledge of my making the cabinets was the same as with the sweat suits. The first thing people wanted to do was fling the doors open and look on the inside. At times, this required me to prepare the wood before I cut it, but the quality was clearly evident upon completion.

Once I designed a cabinet and the lady said, "This is not a piece of furniture, this is a work of art." My chest stuck out in pride. Because of those days spent at home with my grandmother, I can build nearly anything found in any store in any part of the world.

I thank God for all of my abilities because I am able to clearly see that all things work together for the good of them who love the Lord and are called according to His purpose.

Carrying this weight of information and ability is not easy, but is a heavy burden to bear. There is a saying that to whom much is given, much is required, and this statement holds true for all of us. We already have, in our minds, the abilities that are needed to accomplish great things. The requirement comes in the form of exposing ourselves and our children to all of the possibilities that lie ahead.

Our brains are like computers. There is a world of information possible, but without a Wi-Fi connection, that information cannot be accessed. I challenge you to find that connection and open up a world where your mind can connect to its real purpose. When you do this, you give back to God that thing He placed in you.

Many times, when I sit and listen to my own music, eat in a kitchen I made, or rest in a bed I designed and constructed, I simply think of the words God spoke after creation,

It is good.

Rodney Dean Boyden

How Great Thou Art

By
Carl Boberg

O Lord my God, When I in awesome wonder,
Consider all the worlds Thy Hands have made;
I see the stars, I hear the rolling thunder,
Thy power throughout the universe displayed.

Then sings my soul, My Saviour God, to Thee,
How great Thou art, How great Thou art.
Then sings my soul, My Saviour God, to Thee,
How great Thou art, How great Thou art!

When through the woods, and forest glades I wander,
And hear the birds sing sweetly in the trees.
When I look down, from lofty mountain grandeur
And see the brook, and feel the gentle breeze.

Then sings my soul, My Saviour God, to Thee,
How great Thou art, How great Thou art.
Then sings my soul, My Saviour God, to Thee,
How great Thou art, How great Thou art!

Chapter Eleven: "Why Me? Why Music?"

As surprising as it may seem, I voluntarily walked away from my first love, music. This meant that I did not sing or play the piano for a very long time. During the silent years of my musical drought, I often heard the voices of others saying "Why not?" and "You should!" and "You could." My reasons for abandoning my calling were valid to me at the time.

Riddled with unreached goals and pure burnout from the chase, I made the decision to set music aside and pursue carpentry full time. At that point, I surmised that design would be my final artistic rendering to the world. Little did I know that I was trying to give up something that could not be given up. The relationship between music and me could not be overlooked.

I don't believe I found music and I don't believe music found me. I believe that God set up a date for us to find each other. I also believe that music was embedded in the DNA of my chromosomal structure. It was not a matter of where we met, but when. We, Music and I, knew immediately that we were made for each other.

Our relationship began when I was about 8 years old. It was a day like every other day and I was playing in the living room as I ran back and forth from the back porch to the kitchen. Mamma was cooking, as usual.

It was as though the connections in my mind had grown together overnight and when I ran by the piano this time, it looked different. As I approached it, while putting my little hands in the air to touch it for the first time, it said "HEY!!" I looked around because I knew that there was nobody there but my grandmother and she was supposed to be in the kitchen cooking. So I tried again to touch it, and it said once more, "HEY RODNEY"!

When I looked at it and the piano looked at me, it said, "Who are you?" and I said, "Who are you?" I finally got the nerve to lay my little paws on the keys once again, and the keys said, "YEA!!" And I said to myself, "WOW, what a sound!!"

I began to bang on the piano each day from that point on. One day, Mamma paused with ears of awareness, knowing that something miraculous was happening in her living room. She watched and listened for a few years and finally asked one day if I wanted to take piano lessons. My answer came out without knowing the true measure of its consequences, but I said, "Yes, Mamma." My grandmother knew from her own experience as a pianist that the banging was much more that just a passing phase. She knew it was to be a relationship that would stand the test of time long after she was gone.

My piano teacher, Mrs. Bessie Smoot, had been well known in the community for years. She had taught other family members as well as many prominent musicians in our city. For all of us who were lucky enough to be in her student lineup, the lessons all began in the same spot.

She would say, "Imagine the five lines and four spaces that make a music staff." It is known in music that the lines have names and the spaces have names also. Early in my music education, she taught us that the lines from bottom to top can be memorized by saying, E- every, G-good, B- boy, D-does, F-fine and the spaces spell out the word F-A-C-E. All of these lessons had a rule that was simple but mandatory. All songs and musical terms and their meanings had to be memorized before moving forward.

 I laugh at how long it took during my lessons at 9 years old to get this, but it took much longer for me to make the correlation to what it would mean to my life and musical ability in a much deeper way. After a few years of this repeated process of learning, I knew that Every Good Boy Does Fine in the FACE of accepting his calling, and this would be mine.

 The lines and spaces of our lives denote the opportunities that come from the ups and downs of living melodiously. For those who understand music in its simplest form, it's nothing but different notes located on a scale, which make different sounds and pitches to create melodies. I believe that the one reason I love music so much can be attributed to the fact that it has always loved me back.

 I am a person who has many notes and many beats that make up who I am as an individual.

My Grandmother's Faith

I appreciate all of my many skills when they are placed together in the correct order. Music proves to be the common denominator in all that I do. My talents are a microcosm of notes that, in order to be effective, need organization. That can prove to be a very difficult song to write.

Just as there are seven repeating white keys on a keyboard, I possess seven skills that repeated in the days, weeks, and months of my existence. Without the correct plan of action, life can't have the intended melody and can end up being a jumbled cacophony of sound and activity.

I have spent much time honing all of my skills — practicing and learning, as does the classical pianist as he or she practices their arpeggios over and over and over again. I pressed different keys by going to different cities, using different talents, just trying to come up with a song that I'd been longing to hear. You see, in my heart, there rings a particular melody and I was still attempting to hear it.

At 50, I realized, that if I would just stop long enough and allow myself to sit down and take in the notes, looking at them for what they really were, I would find that the melodies are made through my interaction with people, which is the very thing that God placed me on earth to do. As a creative being, it has been very easy to sequester myself in music studios and sound rooms of creation for weeks at a time. Most people have no idea how much time I actually spend alone in a creative space and mode. But as the arms of time moved round and round, I came to realize that I have nothing if I don't share the results of that time to bring joy and happiness to those who hear it.

When I put music away, it had not dawned on me that I was putting down something in a way that would not only hurt me, but deprive others who understood the importance of it and how special I am to even make it "do what it do," as they say.

When I put music away, I was putting down my very soul.

When I put music away, I was putting down the very thing that makes me who I am and what God created me to be.

Even though the piano lid of my musical mind was shut, the strings still vibrated in my head and I could hear them calling me in many different ways.

How could I give up something with which I had enjoyed a passionate love affair for more than 40 years? I know it is impossible to imagine, but music was interfering with my ability to accomplish all my other talents. I was traveling and doing all of the things you have read about in this book while music was getting in my way.

It wasn't until I began to do something very unusual and unscripted that I would find the turning point to the healing of this old forgotten relationship. I reflected upon the simplest form of music and started talking to my friends on Facebook about it. There, I played the songs that meant so much to me from my childhood. These were the old, forgotten Hymns that were discarded and thrown away. The muted creation of the ages. The boring melodies that are too long and word-driven. Yes, The Hymn.

Hymns have been the way by which we have been coming together in churches across the world in common melody for centuries. The hymn is something that is embedded in the hearts and minds of people who have had the church experience for any amount of time. It is the sound of my grandmother. It is the sound of voices ringing and moving over old wooden pews in chapels throughout the world. It is a sound unlike any other.

The hymns were the first gospel music I read at 9 years old in Sunday school. I recalled when my pastor, Reverend Robert I. Brown, would turn around in his deep voice and say, "What a friend We have in Jesus," I was happy because that was a song that I could play really well.

It is amazing that at 48 when I began to play again, I didn't start with Richard Smallwood, John P. Key or the wonderful music of the Clark sisters and Walter Hawkins. The hymn medley I played on a video that would be viewed by over 1.2 million people on my Facebook page would be, yes, you guessed it, "What A Friend We Have in Jesus."

It is the hymn in which music and melody are simple in their structures, and the chords were triads with flowing octave base lines. For some reason, I wanted to go back to the basics, where people could understand and get a new respect and a new perspective of something that was old.

The amazing thing that I want to convey is an undeniable fact. When I started with no need to impress, no need to follow the masses, repeating the sounds and runs of the new voice, I was delivering to the masses the core of who I really was musically. Once I began to touch the piano again, sharing tidbits of many hymns for the listeners, I noticed that my friend request light lit up each day with new people from all walks of life, from all over the world, who shared my love for this music.

I went from 2000 friends to 5000 on one page and started an overflow page for the new listeners and friends. Including the followers, this music shows itself in the form of over 20,000 people listening each time I post one of these wonderful songs, within just a few weeks.

It is the hymn in its simple melody and scripture of song put to music that calls the recognizing ear to run where the melody resides. The relationship that I have with music is not predicated on a sophisticated playing style. It was not the flawless, melodious styling of my voice nor was it the clothes I was wearing. It was not the grooming of my facial hair and it surely wasn't about the untuned spinnets, uprights and grand pianos that I was playing as I traveled around the country.

None of that mattered to the listeners, but it was the emotion and the sanctity of the communication of my hands touching the 88 black and white keys. It was the singing and playing songs that everybody could identify with. Black, white, Asian, Indian and many more write regularly asking about different songs and styles and expressing their interest in learning more and more about it. There are people who even ask me to teach them how to play this music. WOW!

This music touches a heart and soul place. It is not just an ear place where the music excites your need to move, clap and dance and show us "what you working with" in church! These songs go back and they reach into your spine as they pull out that grandmother's voice. I remember being in church as a child and all of a sudden Mamma would chime in. It was the morning hymn that so abruptly woke me up out of an angelic sleep as I laid on her lap. Holy Holy Holy, Lord God Almighty.

These are the songs that make you go back and understand who you are and what you're made of. Just when I started to do this, there was something that I heard in a sanctified place that spoke clearly to me. Do exactly what you are doing, just the way you're doing it because there are many people that are being blessed by the simplicity of the sound that you are providing.

This is not a sound or a style that is provided by many today, but for those who do it, when people hear it, many can identify with the sound. When I reached the place where I stopped coveting others' musical styles, and began to share my gift freely, then the melody of my music began to pollinate the lives of others. When this happens, I can sit on the porch of life and appreciate what I've been given.

Sometimes the music of today is so jazzy that it flies over the head of the people in the congregation. The musicians are so into what they are playing, that they don't take any time to notice that 75 percent of the crowd is not effected or affected by any of it. I purposefully watch this as I travel and visit churches across the nation.

It is fun to watch the musicians hit a certain chord. The music pit jerks in affirmation while the poor choir is struggling to hear the person right next to them. The women and the mics are screeching trying to be heard over the piercing sound of the organ, drums and other instruments being played.

It's not for the listener, but the music at that point is for the musicians. The congregants can't understand a single word that is being sung and they sit there perplexed. I can see the founding member of The First Baptist Church of the Lord God Almighty Community Apostolic Association as she sits there wondering when in the world did this happen to what we used to call church music. In some cases, today's music is not reaching any part of their hearts, minds or souls. I have found that people need to feel a connection between the melodies, the music and the words so that they can be fed through song.

The well-rounded musician will be better served to create a atmosphere where hymns along with contemporary music can be shared equally during the worship experience.

So when I say "Why Me and Why Music," it took all of these years for me to come to know that I had been chosen to present this music not just for my own enjoyment at home where I can't be heard, but also for me to share with the masses that they might connect again. This music is for them to get a closer relationship with God.

The songs are peaceful, meaningful and the melodies of the music are smooth and sweet. They cause them to go to a place where they can sit down for once in their lives. It is wonderful to have quiet time and sing words like "Master the tempest is raging the billows are tossing high," "He's sweet I know, storm clouds may rise and strong winds may blow, I can tell the world wherever I may go that I found a savior and he's sweet I know."

I know that this music is just for those people who need a message from God. These songs don't need a beat to be effective because they were not created with kick drums, snares, Roland pianos or Motif EX-8s. These songs were shared in a spiritual, sanctified and lyrically liturgical thought process. When you hear a hymn, you know that you are not in the club, but you are in Church.

There was a little lady that always said, "If you don't use it, you're going to lose it." To her I say today, "It is only because of God's grace and his mercy that has kept me and allowed me to return to the very thing that he knows I Love. I will never leave it again."

Music is the place where I am supposed to be sitting at those 88 black and white keys that make up the melody of my life. I know that I can do all things through Christ who strengthens me. This means, I can do carpentry, I can be an artist, I can be a tailor, AND I CAN be a musician and singer because they are ALL a part of my life as I sing the familiar hymn.

My Grandmother's Faith

Jesus is All the World to Me

By
Will L. Thompson

Jesus is all the world to me,
My life, my joy, my all.
He is my strength from day to day;
Without Him I would fall.
When I am sad, to Him I go;
No other one can cheer me so.
When I am sad, He makes me glad;
He's my Friend.

Jesus is all the world to me,
My Friend in trials sore.
I go to Him for blessings, and
He gives them o'er and o'er.
He sends the sunshine and the rain;
He sends the harvest's golden grain:
Sunshine and rain, harvest of grain—
He's my Friend.

Jesus is all the world to me,
And true to Him I'll be.
Oh, how could I this Friend deny
When He's so true to me?
Following Him I know I'm right;
He watches o'er me day and night.
Following Him by day and night,
He's my Friend.

Rodney Dean Boyden

Jesus is all the world to me,
I want no better friend.
I trust Him now; I'll trust Him when
Life's fleeting days shall end.
Beautiful life with such a Friend;
Beautiful life that has no end!
Eternal life, eternal joy,
He's my Friend.

Chapter Twelve: Mamma's Legacy

Many people are confused about the true definition of unconditional love. They are unable to fully comprehend what it is and how it makes a difference. To love unconditionally is to simply love a person for who they are, not for what they can do or have done. It is not based on the past, present, or future. The person who is able to really love is perfectly settled within himself or herself and chooses to give love without any expectations of love being returned.

1 Corinthians 13:4-7 spells out the breadth and width of love's attributes. It says that love

is patient and kind. It does not envy, it does not boast, it is not proud. It does not dishonor others, it is not self-seeking, it is not easily angered, and it keeps no record of wrongs. Love does not delight in evil but rejoices with the truth. It always protects, always trusts, always hopes, and always perseveres. *My Grandmother's Faith* is a legacy of unconditional love.

Not long ago, someone asked me, "What if people don't have a person like your grandmother in their life to pour into them as she did you?" That question caused me to think back on other people, in addition to my grandmother, who had made a positive difference in my life. It also brought back memories of young lives that I hopefully impacted in a positive way.

Years ago, while serving as an inner city elementary school music teacher, there was one student who always gave me a bit of pushback. He just could not follow the rules in class. I stayed on him, even though at times I didn't think I was reaching him. Nevertheless, we made it to the end of the year.

Due to poor attendance, the end of the school year's PTA performance was a very discouraging event for me. The parents in that area did not see the importance of coming to the events themselves, or bringing their children.

However, this little boy came without his parents. He sang with his little face covered with the lollipop he had enjoyed on the walk to the school. After the performance he came to me and said, "Mr. Boyden, I appreciate you." The pure shock that came over me was not evident because I could not react. It affected me deeply because after all, I was the teacher.

I said, "Really, why do you appreciate me?" He said, "I appreciate you because you stayed on me all year and you didn't let me do what I wanted to do." I understood exactly what he meant. As tears welled up in my eyes, all I could do was kneel down and hug the little sixth grader. I hugged him so that he would not see that his words had busted my insides wide open.

There are many stories like this where I went to the extreme to show the kids that I wanted a certain outcome in my classroom. I always reminded them that I had been a child myself, and whatever they were thinking about doing in my class, I had already done it, and it did not turn out well for me. Most of them listened most of the time.

On yet another day in music class, someone else attempted to disrupt my class. Much to his complete surprise and shock, I leaped straight up and over the middle of the high back console piano I was playing and landed right in front of the disruptive student. I informed this child of his need to exit the room immediately because Mr. Boyden was NOT HAVING IT! Now I laugh at the thought, because I was around 29 years of age then, but today, at 50 years old, my days of piano jumping are almost over.

To this day, students from that class recall the time that I did what they considered the unthinkable. I did it so they could see that I, one of only a few black men that they would even see in that school system, cared enough to even be there working with them. I did it so that they could see I cared enough about their ability to sit and learn without interruption.

I did it so they could see another teaching style and understand that they could not try that with Mr. Boyden, Because He Is Crazy but he DOES CARE!!!

Every time I see my old students, who are now between 30 and 35 years old, they remind me of those days, and it makes me proud. They let me know that as a teacher, I left an imprint on their minds. And they love me because I gave them that extra push to not only succeed, but to exceed expectations.

These are just a few examples of the things that kids need from us. They need visible signs of how it is supposed to be. My grandmother loved me unconditionally in my life's journey and we must love the youth in the same way. Whatever happened to the days when it was good to tell someone else's child that the path that they were traveling was wrong? Whatever happened to the days when we could call and inform parents of their child's actions and they would push aside the thought that their baby would never be as you described? Involvement is the answer!

Kids need involvement from people outside of the home who have skills, jobs, and words to share. This input cannot happen at 20, 19, 18, or 17 years old. It has to happen at 8, 9, 10, 11 years old.

To use my own community as an example, every day I see young boys who have no purpose and drive towards any particular thing. They have no skills to show and no awareness of their own innate ability. They cannot imagine anything but hanging on the corner or getting the new tennis shoe or watches. For most, if it is not football or basketball, it does not get their attention.

This is the age where, in my experience, the mind of a child begins to really understand possibilities. They begin to catch on to a subject or activity that fits them. The only way this can take place is if they are exposed to much more through the people who live it successfully each day. They need to see positive role models who drive nice cars, have nice things, do good things and are great people in the community through their hard work and skill.

A man without skill is destined to head down a path of negativity and uselessness, because his mind is not occupied with the thought of action. His mind is not in the mode of problem-solving, product creation, machine acclimation, imagination and implementation.

Kids can have the experience that I just shared in this book; this can happen when we all take a part of the responsibility to involve ourselves in a positive way to educate, motivate and acclimate them to all of the possibilities that exist in the world.

My grandmother was not one of a kind. She was not the only grandmother or person who loved to this degree. There are millions of them all over the world who give themselves every day in many ways.

Those who made a difference in my world were people like the lady on the street in town who smiled at me; it was the man in the hardware store who took the time to show me something I had never seen. It was grass man "Oscar," who came to cut the back yard and sat me up on his tractor, explaining how the blades turned to cut weeds and bushes. It was my family, who showed me through hard work, that you can live a good, solid life. It was the Sunday school teacher who would share her love and God's love in Church. It was that piece of peppermint candy shared by an old lady sitting next to us for the first time.

My views came through many people of different races, and from many places. So, when I was asked the question, "What if people don't have a person like your grandmother in their life?" the reason for this book became evident.

Sharing Mamma's love and examples of support and affirmation enables this unconditional love to be adopted by anyone who reads the pages. Her love can be put into action with that little child you see at church or at school or at play.

The child who you know has the knack and light of creativity for something greater than himself.

My grandmother's faith is embodied in a literary work titled, "Equipment" by Edgar A. Guest. This was also Dr. George Washington Carver's favorite poem. I can imagine this former slave turned scientist walking around laboratories at the great Tuskegee Institute reciting the poem as he invented many products from peanuts and sweet potatoes.

I suppose that my affinity with the poem is due to the fact that I share its powerful ideology, and in my own creative way, have sought to prove its truth through varied pursuits. I am fascinated by the impression that it leaves on the canvas of my mind each time I read it.

> Figure it out for yourself, my lad,
> You've all that the greatest of men have had,
> Two arms, two hands, two legs, two eyes
> And a brain to use if you would be wise.
> With this equipment they all began,
> So start for the top and say, "I can."
>
> Look them over, the wise and great
> They take their food from a common plate,
> And similar knives and forks they use,
> With similar laces they tie their shoes.
> The world considers them brave and smart,
> But you've all they had when they made their start.

My Grandmother's Faith

> You can triumph and come to skill,
> You can be great if you only will.
> You're well equipped for what fight you choose,
> You have legs and arms and a brain to use,
> And the man who has risen great deeds to do
> Began his life with no more than you.
>
> You are the handicap you must face,
> You are the one who must choose your place,
> You must say where you want to go,
> How much you will study the truth to know.
> God has equipped you for life, but He
> Lets you decide what you want to be.
>
> Courage must come from the soul within,
> The man must furnish the will to win.
> So figure it out for yourself, my lad.
> You were born with all that the great have had,
> With your equipment they all began,
> Get hold of yourself and say: "I can."

I encourage you to reach for skills that can help build your life, community, and your world. You will see that your presence is valid, accepted and needed, and the light in your soul will shine with pride. You will then give as you give, walk as you walk, love as you love, but most of all, you will feel that hug of My Grandmother's Faith as it wraps you up in the grasp of God's will and plan for your lives. Love a child today, because your life and their life depends on it.

Rodney Dean Boyden
Pauline's baby

Epilogue: Finding Normal

As I complete this writing project and coast towards the finish line of the process, I am led to share what Paul Harvey, a newscaster from back in the day, called "The Rest of the Story." Recently, I called one of my favorite cousins to discuss all of the things that are going on with the world. Due to his training and expertise on the topics of my concern, he shared some interesting points that helped clear up a lot of things for me.

Our conversation went from one thing to another until we finally landed on life, work and retirement. He shared with me that in the early days of his retirement, he and his family went through a readjustment period because everyone had to adjust to Dad being around all day.

I, being Rodney, made a statement that sparked a larger narrative. I told him that I wanted to live a normal life like him. He said, "Rodney, I cannot recall a time when your life was normal." He went on to say that since my many talents had kept me on the road for more than fifteen years, he didn't know if it was possible for me to be normal. He said that all of my years of traveling and working from one city to the next, for months at a time, perplexed his mind.

As he talked, I listened. I thought about the fact that he had retired after one very successful career, and was working on a second one. In addition to all of that, he had a wife, two beautiful girls, and a big house. In my mind, his life was good. As he described the attributes of his life and how it all worked, my brain raced to find any similarity between his reality and my own.

It made me laugh to think that if someone were to do an MRI on my brain to search for signals of normal, the results on the chart would come back "no findings," because normal takes on a new meaning when you are a person like me. Abnormality is my Normality.

Most guys go to school, get a job, get married, have kids, buy a house, get a dog, lay back in a recliner, and drink Cokes while waiting for dinner to get ready each evening. They also have kids jumping around, screaming and shouting, wives complaining, dogs barking, and cable that occasionally doesn't work.

All of these are normal and acceptable activities for those who saw it first-hand in their childhood experiences. However, while growing up, my normal was a traveling grandfather who lived in another state. Going to and fro, back and forth, in and out: he loved that life. He was able to have the best of both worlds. I watched this and it set an example of continuous motion as the rule of the day. It seemed to work for my grandparents, so why would it not work for me? Up until this point, the thought process of continuous motion had ruled my every decision.

I told my cousin that the greatest level of peace and happiness I had ever experienced was when serving a church as Minister of Music. I explained further that it gave me the chance to live a normal life for once, with a paycheck, office, and all that came with it. I even loved the repeated drive to get there each day on the newly constructed highway. I remember the car that this normalcy afforded me as I cruised to work in my black Mercedes, listening to the music. I was in hog heaven.

The difference between hogs and me was that the hogs knew when they had it good. They were happy right where they were ... eating slop, rolling around in the mud, and looking at the ducks as they sat each day getting fat just for us. Unlike hogs, though, I just could not sit still. I had the "get up and go spirit" engrained within me. I was normal once. My undoing was an oxymoron of opportunity that pulled me away from routine living.

Can we allow what we consider amazing opportunities to pull us away from what we are supposed to be doing? The answer is yes, because sometimes those opportunities might be masked in a cloak of happiness that can derail your forward motion. For this reason, you should always think long and hard about the so-called "amazing opportunities" that come your way.

I did not always have this wisdom, so I offer it as advice because of a bad decision that I made. I took the bait of walking down another path. It was a road that seemed to be a shortcut to greatness, but it proved to be a meandering path of crisscrossing deals and jobs that I now reflect on as pit stops for wasting time.

To me, it is like mapping out a three-day trip direct from New York to California for an event. Because of my adventurous spirit, I stop at every sight-seeing spot along the way, not following the plan. Now this three-day trip turns into 15 exhausting days and missing the event for which the trip was meant.

If you have ever heard the adage, "Plan your work, work your plan," I was the king of the first part and the second part proved to be the challenge. Even though I took lessons while traveling this road, it took me years to realize that I just needed to get back to the main highway.

Did I learn things while wasting time? Yes, I did. Did I do any good while wasting time? Yes, I did. Did I meet great people while wasting time? Sure, I did. However, no matter how I want to fix it, I was wasting time. This idea of wasted time is hard to understand for those who ascribe to the "follow your dreams" mentality.

I ask, if you are one of these people, to take my life and glean just a few things from it. I can't live the last 20 years over again, but I can show you just a few ways how living a dream can affect your effectiveness.

When my road of abnormality crossed normal, it showed in many ways, one being the search for a wife. I tried to find one, but it didn't work, because the ladies were in the normal lane and I was bad, cool, and slick while driving in the express lane.

Frequently, I went too fast, wasted too much gas, and burned out the engine of my body trying to keep up as if I was on the Autobahn of life's adventures. The ladies looked at me and said to themselves, "Go on fool, kill yourself," and "I'll be here when you get back, if you make it back." Since I am still single, even Ray Charles and Helen Keller can see that I have not made it back.

It also showed in a son that I didn't take the time to raise, just as my own father had done. One particular conversation I had with my son is forever etched in my mind. When I asked how he felt about me and all that had happened, he replied, "I don't have any reason to hate you, and I'm here if you want me in your life, but if you don't, I will be okay too, because this is your normal."

My piercing reality, to say the least, was sitting right in front of me, looking just like me, telling me about myself. What a strong young man he is. The fact that my own son has been able to stay on the road that leads toward fortitude and purpose without me is a blessing from Almighty God. My son shows me that normal does work.

My grandmother's faith and her love is the only reason that I have been able to survive in this space of abnormality for such a long period. If the light from my time with her had not been shining from the lighthouse of my childhood, I would not have remembered normal or how to get back to it. Even in all of this moving to and fro, I still have the chance to get back to finding normal. What it will look like is very eye opening and I have come to grips with how best to achieve it.

The scripture that supports my decision is found in 1 Corinthians 15:58. It says, "Therefore, my dear brothers and sisters, stand firm. Let nothing move you. Always give yourselves fully to the work of the Lord, because you know that your labor in the Lord is not in vain."

I have adopted this passage as the GPS of my new direction. It speaks to me clearly as it directs my next move. The next move is no move at all! In my attempt to live in this space of normalcy that most of you enjoy, I must come down off the pedestal of constant activity, self-gratification, impulsiveness, and self-imposed loneliness in order to enjoy all of the blessings that are waiting there.

I feel confident that standing firm on this ideal will manifest itself into a life of fulfilled dreams and peaceful days drinking tea and eating chicken wings in the rocking chair of God's provision. As my cousin accepted his retirement, I accept my new path. God has promised that if I am steadfast and just stop moving, all He has for me is located in that simple place.

As I look at the plight of young men today and all that is going on, I know that I must share these experiences with them for many reasons. I want them to see the effects of not having a plan for their lives early on, and how just setting goals and sticking to them can lead to a great life. "Great" is a relative term for each person, and it is much better than looking over your shoulder in fear each day.

The fear of not knowing, the fear of insecurity, the fear of trying to fit in and the fear of no direction is guiding them and I need to share my talents and skills with them so that they can see a way out of this mindset.

The words from the following poem, "If" by Rudyard Kipling, reminds me that my mind can calm my body.

> If you can keep your head when all about you
> Are losing theirs and blaming it on you;
> If you can trust yourself when all men doubt you,
> But make allowance for their doubting too:
> If you can wait and not be tired by waiting,
> Or, being lied about, don't deal in lies,
> Or being hated don't give way to hating,
> And yet don't look too good, nor talk too wise;
>
> If you can dream - and not make dreams your master;
> If you can think - and not make thoughts your aim,

My Grandmother's Faith

If you can meet with Triumph and Disaster
And treat those two impostors just the same:.
If you can bear to hear the truth you've spoken
Twisted by knaves to make a trap for fools,
Or watch the things you gave your life to, broken,
And stoop and build'em up with worn-out tools;

If you can make one heap of all your winnings
And risk it on one turn of pitch-and-toss,
And lose, and start again at your beginnings,
And never breathe a word about your loss:
If you can force your heart and nerve and sinew
To serve your turn long after they are gone,
And so hold on when there is nothing in you
Except the Will which says to them: "Hold on!"

If you can talk with crowds and keep your virtue,
Or walk with Kings - nor lose the common touch,
If neither foes nor loving friends can hurt you,
If all men count with you, but none too much:
If you can fill the unforgiving minute
With sixty seconds' worth of distance run,
Yours is the Earth and everything that's in it,
And - which is more - you'll be a Man, my son!

Rodney Dean Boyden

I Surrender All

Judson W. Van Deventer

All to Jesus I surrender,
All to Him I freely give;
I will ever love and trust Him,
In His presence daily live.

Refrain:
I surrender all,
I surrender all;
All to Thee, my blessed Savior,
I surrender all.

All to Jesus I surrender,
Humbly at His feet I bow;
Worldly pleasures all forsaken,
Take me, Jesus, take me now.

All to Jesus I surrender,
Make me, Savior, wholly Thine;
Let me feel the Holy Spirit,
Truly know that Thou art mine.

All to Jesus I surrender,
Lord, I give myself to Thee;
Fill me with Thy love and power,
Let Thy blessing fall on me.

All to Jesus I surrender,
Now I feel the sacred flame;
Oh, the joy of full salvation!
Glory, glory, to His Name!

My Grandmother's Faith

*Mrs. Pauline C. Boyden
1913 to 1993*

Rodney Dean Boyden

Dear Mamma

This letter is a continuation of the one that I stuck in your casket before I closed the lid so many years ago.

Thank you for inspiring me to be the person that I am today. I tell people that if they like me, thank my grandmother, and if you don't like me, blame my grandmother. Of course that is just a joke, because there is no blame in you.

You gave me the very best that you had to offer, and you gave me your heart.

Anytime I go through life and do something wonderful, you are the first person I think of, and any time that I have problems and have down days, I think of you and remember the times we spent together. That gets me through my day.

I know that you think you might be forgotten, but you know that my heart beats every day because of you.

I am able to love people because of you. Sometimes because of you, it's hard for me to love because they are not you and that is a challenge but, I appreciate you for setting up a bar that is, in some cases, hard to reach for others.

My Grandmother's Faith

I thank you for being a Godsend and I appreciate you for your good decisions and sometimes unpopular decisions.

I appreciate you for pushing me and holding my hands when others talked about me.

I appreciate you for holding me when I was crying and cleaning up the blood when I fell and busted my head on my bike three and four times. I do not forgive you for letting Daddy make me wear that football helmet while riding my bike. I can't let that one slide. LOL!

I appreciate you for sitting behind me at piano lessons for 11 years and sacrificing for me to have the best in all things.

I appreciate all those walks to the laundromat and all the times we hung clothes on the line together.

I appreciate you for allowing me to be the little man when daddy died. You let me cut the grass without watching me, even though I would imagine you were peeking out the window making sure I was okay.

I appreciate you for telling me to go pick up apples and making apple pies when we got them off the tree.

I appreciate you for setting the example of what a woman should be and what I should seek in a mate, even though sometimes difficult.

I appreciate you for holding my hand and rubbing my head when I would come home.

I appreciate when you would wash my hair in the bathroom sink and at the end of it you would press down on my head to ring out the rag water on my head. I looked forward to that press every time.

I remember when you were in the hospital bed for years sick and needing help. I remember how I would look at you when I came home, knowing that you would be there.

I remember the motor of your lift chair, when I knew that you were on the move.

I knew that you were there and you wanted to move.

I remember taking you to get ice cream when you were sick. I took you for a ride to Grandview State Park just so that you could look at your favorite flower which is the rhododendron. I remember when I came back out of the place from getting your ice cream, because you were not strong enough, you had slid down in the seat of the car. All I could see was your hat and how we both laughed all the way home as you ate your ice cream cone. What a wonderful day that was just riding through the beautiful mountains of West Virginia, just you and me.

I remember all of those things.

I remember the day that I had to walk away from you.

I remember it and I remember saying, "I love this woman and I need this woman, but I can live on and walk on strong knowing that this woman existed and that this woman loved me and that I am an extension of all that she implanted and imparted in me, knowingly and unknowingly."

> For every time I sing a note,
> For every time I play a note.
> For every time I build a room.
> For every time I draw a picture.
> For every time I paint a picture.
> For every time I speak in public.
> For every time I'm on television.
> For every time I'm on the pulpit.
> I am a reflection of you.

Years ago, I purchased a music project by my favorite female artist, Roberta Flack. On this project was a song called, "You Brought Me Love." When this song played in rotation on my many travels, I cried thinking of you and changed the words to fit my feelings. This song is for us.

Rodney Dean Boyden

You Who Brought Me Love

Adapted from Roberta Flack's original recording

Mamma you brought me love
You gave me peace of mind
And never asking for anything back
You changed my life

Mamma you brought me hope
You gave me reason to try
For once it's my turn to show you
You'll always be the only one

You gave me all you've got
It's you who brought me love
Mamma I'll take your hand
Through the roughest of times

And I'll be here for you
Like you've been here for me
A thousand times
I'll do just as you've done

For you who brought me love
It's you who brought me love
How many times
In new life do you find

A Mamma who's a loving friend
Never asking for anything more
Both there in the end
Now I touch your face

My Grandmother's Faith

Holding you to mine
Knowing we've got tomorrow
And for all we've come through
We'll get by

These words won't say enough
I've nothing here but love
For you who brought me love
It's you brought me love

It's you who brought me love
Who brought me love
Who brought me love

Rodney Dean Boyden

Had I Not Been

Had I not been born as a college baby, I would not have been adopted by my grandparents.

Had I not been adopted by my grandparents, I would have never had the undivided attention of a loving grandmother who provided all of the tools that I needed to explore life, art, and complete creativity.

Had I not explored creativity, I would not have learned how to play piano, sing, draw, paint, sew, and understand shapes like I did by the early age of 13.

Had I not explored my gifts, I would not have been given the chance to play my first songs in the Sunday School of Central Baptist Church under the watchful eye of Robert I. Brown and learn to sing and project in front of large crowds.

Had I not learned those early skills, I would not have moved to Charleston, WV to play for many churches and choirs learning more skills in all types of music.

Had I not learned those skills, I would not have been chosen by Bishop T.D. Jakes to become the first Assistant Minister of Music of The Potter's House in Dallas, Texas.

Here is where it gets really good!

Had I not been in that Music position, I would not have made the biggest mistake of my life!

Had I not made the biggest mistake of my life, I would not have moved to play for a small church in the "Hood" where I met Bishop Frazier and his wonderful Family who held me up until I got my mind back.

Had I not been supported in that way, I would have never been ready to accept the new position as Minister of Music of one of the largest UMC Churches in Dallas. Had I not been there in that position, I would have never met Floyd Jones, who, in one 30-minute tool training session, taught me the specifics of the world of carpentry and all that was possible through the little things required in the precision of cutting wood.

Had I not met him, I would not have been in Atlanta, Georgia working on a house and been chosen out of over 7000 carpenters from around the country to be on HGTV, making it through 5-6 episodes and finally being the helper of the winner! Had I not done that, I would not have been chosen to do some of the coolest projects for some of America's greatest people and families.

Had I not been working for those families, I would not have been in the right city to be chosen to sing for and shake the hand of the President of the United States of America during one of his visits!

Had I not been there, I would not have been in the mind of my newest customer. Had I not done that, I would not be sitting here in New Jersey writing this letter as I prepare for this project completion.

What does all this mean? It means that I can not be discouraged by my mistakes, because those very things that I thought would be my end can be credited for leading me to my life's greater and more fulfilling purpose! The truth is that had any one of these events not occurred, the trajectory of my life would look a whole lot differently.

Biography

Rodney Dean Boyden is a native of Beckley, West Virginia. He graduated from Woodrow Wilson High School in 1984. After many years of church music experience and over a decade of private piano lessons, he went on to study music at West Virginia State University. He is an accomplished vocalist, pianist, visual artist, interior designer, furniture designer, builder, clothing designer and tailor.

In the 1980s, Rodney was a frequent contestant on the Apollo Theater stage where he won 5th, 2nd, and 1st place on the weekly Wednesday Night Amateur Competition.

Rodney was a well-known pianist for many churches in the area around Beckley and Charleston, West Virginia. He was an itinerate music teacher for 12 elementary school choirs in the Kanawha County School System. In 1996 he was chosen by Bishop T.D. Jakes to serve as the first Assistant Minister of Music for The Potter's House Church in Dallas, Texas. His smooth vocals are featured on the title song of the Grammy-nominated Potter's House Choir album entitled "The Storm Is Over Now," which he performed at the Stellar Awards with Bishop T. D. Jakes and Mrs. Beverly Crawford.

Rodney has also performed on stage with other gospel music artists such as Kirk Franklin, Fred Hammond, and Donnie McClurkin. As a musical guest, he has been frequently featured on Trinity Broadcasting Network's nationally broadcast television shows "Praise The Lord" and "Unfolding Majesties" with Dean and Mary Brown. He was also chosen to perform the Star Spangled Banner for President Barack Obama's visit to Charleston, West Virginia in 2016.

He was the lead male character acting in the popular stage play "Woman, Thou Art Loosed," produced by T.D. Jakes and directed by Tyler Perry. He was also employed as the personal assistant to Tyler Perry and wardrobe specialist for the stage play "Madea's Class Reunion."

Rodney's creativity is not limited to the musical arts, but includes both the visual and the performing arts. In 1999, he entered the field of carpentry. Developing skills as a furniture designer and master builder, he began designing and building residential kitchens, bathrooms, room additions as well as visual sets for theater productions from Atlanta to California.

Rodney was chosen as one of 10 contestants out of 6,000 applicants to appear as a contestant on the third season of "All American Handyman," which aired on Home & Garden Television (HGTV).

Rodney is the owner of Boyden Interior Designs in Dallas, Texas and travels throughout the country creating unique, custom designs for his clients. He is also well known for designing home interior accents including drapes, pillows and upholstery as well as visual interior artist pieces and much more. You can see more of his work at www.rodneyboyden.com.

He is famous for his unique off-the-cuff designs that combine artful style and superior function. His innovative new slanted edged stage design can be seen at The Potter's House sanctuary in Dallas, Texas.

He is a custom tailor known for his personal clothing design and tailoring. He lent his tailoring abilities to Kirk Franklin and family, where he was commissioned to make his children's clothing for the Hero album sleeve. He also was responsible for the original design of the dress for Mrs. Beverly Crawford's Stellar Award performance.

His latest endeavor has taken him back to his first love of Gospel music and hymns. His videos have been viewed over 2.5 million times since November of 2015.

As an author and up and coming playwright, he aspires to share his talents with the youth of the world to rebuild self-esteem and validation. He says, "My first 50 years was for me, but my next 50 years is for them."

My Grandmother's Faith

Just Me